R.S. Thomas:
Letters to Raymond Garlick
1951–1999

Letter 126, R.S.T says Jesus
was a pacifist but Jesus
was not.

"DyLan Thomas a bad influence" P. 29

P.99 "Aberdaron must be one of the most
ignorant and obsequious parts of the
country." Christmas 1976

P.131 "While I was a priest I tried to
promote peace in my parishes." 1988

P.18 R.S. on Dylan Thomas – "a few major lyrics"

P.29 "Dylan Thomas – he is a bad influence
He wrote a half-dozen first-class lyrics
– the rest is dross."

Aberdaron.

Dear Raymond

Here are my poor Christmas
wishes. a warm offering from a cold
heart. A Christian has no right to be
despondent, but there is a chill in the
air out of the future.

I am retiring at Easter. I shall be 65.
I could stay till 70, but I am glad
to go from a Church I no longer
believe in, sycophantic to the queen,
iconoclastic with language, changing
for the sake of change and regardless
of beauty. The Christian structure is
a meaningful structure, but in the hands
of theologians or the common people it is
a poor thing.

You will know that a group of us
have formed a trust to buy Bardsey. We
have signed the contract, but are going to
have to raise £200,000 to pay for it and run
it. So we are going to have a job to preserve
its character of peace and seclusion.

I hope you have good news of Destyn
and Angharad. Gyda chyfarchion
Ronald

R.S. Thomas's letter to Raymond Garlick, Christmas 1977

R.S. Thomas:
Letters to Raymond Garlick
1951–1999

Edited, with an Introduction and Notes, by

Jason Walford Davies

Gomer

828.99291

Published in 2009 by
Gomer Press, Llandysul, Ceredigion, SA44 4JL

ISBN 978 1 84323 826 3
A CIP record for this title is available from the British Library.

© text of R. S. Thomas's letters: Kunjana Thomas 2001
© text of Raymond Garlick's letter: Raymond Garlick
© Introduction and editorial matter: Jason Walford Davies

This book is published with the financial support of the
Welsh Books Council.

 Arts & Humanities
Research Council

Printed and bound in Wales at
Gomer Press, Llandysul, Ceredigion

Contents

Acknowledgements   vii

Editor's Note   ix

Introduction: A Corresponding Voice   xi

R.S. Thomas: 'Commission: *for Raymond Garlick*'   lvii

The Letters, 1951–1999   1

Notes and References   159

Appendix:
Raymond Garlick's Only Surviving Letter to R.S. Thomas   203

Acknowledgements

Grateful acknowledgement for permission to quote from the poetry of R.S. Thomas is due to the following: Gwydion Thomas, Kunjana Thomas, and Rhodri Thomas; M. Wynn Thomas; and Bloodaxe Books. Quotations from *R.S. Thomas: Autobiographies* (1997), translated and edited by Jason Walford Davies, are used by kind permission of J.M. Dent, a division of The Orion Publishing Group. For permission to quote from the work of Raymond Garlick I am grateful to Raymond Garlick himself and Gwasg Gomer.

Quotations from the following are used by kind permission of Faber and Faber Ltd: Lawrence Durrell's 'Letters in Darkness', from *Collected Poems 1931–1974* (1985); T.S. Eliot's 'Gerontion', 'Little Gidding' and *The Waste Land*, from *Collected Poems 1909–1962* (1963); Ted Hughes's 'Famous Poet', from *The Hawk in the Rain* (1957); Ezra Pound's *Pisan Cantos* LXXXI, from *The Cantos* (1975).

John Wain's 'Green Fingers: To Elizabeth Jennings in Oxford', from *Letters to Five Artists* (1969), is quoted by kind permission of Macmillan Ltd.

Twm Morys's poem 'R.S.', from *2* (2002), is quoted by kind permission of the poet, Alan Llwyd and Cyhoeddiadau Barddas.

This volume was completed with the aid of a grant from the Arts & Humanities Research Council (AHRC) under their Research Leave Scheme, for which I am grateful.

I would also like to thank the following: John Barnie, Carys Briddon, Tony Brown, Garech Browne, Patrick Crotty, Iestyn Daniel, Ceri Davies, Gareth Emanuel, Mary Evans, Peter Finch, Elin ap Hywel, Dylan Iorwerth, Ceri Wyn Jones,

Dafydd Glyn Jones, Mairwen Prys Jones, Peter Hope Jones, Patrick McGuinness, Morag Law, Gwyneth Lewis, William R. Lewis, Robin Llywelyn, Kevin Perryman, Dylan Phillips, Huw Pryce, Guto Prys, Rhian Reynolds, John Rowlands, Marc Rowlands, Lleucu Siencyn, Fraser Steel, M. Wynn Thomas, Angharad Tomos, Robat Trefor, Helen Wilcox. I am very grateful to Damian Walford Davies and Meinir Lloyd Davies for their support and advice.

My main thanks go to Raymond Garlick himself, to whom I am especially grateful for his kindness and assistance.

Jason Walford Davies

Editor's Note

The layout and punctuation of the address at the head of each letter, and the position of the date, together with the punctuation of the initial greeting and the sign-off in each case, have been standardized throughout. The text of the letters has been kept as in the original, apart from the correction of minor lapses and the necessary excision of personal material. For the sake of clarity and consistency, the county names used in the Notes and References are the historical ones, as given in the *Dictionary of the Place-Names of Wales* (2007).

R.S. Thomas's poems are quoted from the original volumes. Where relevant, a poem's location in Thomas's *Collected Poems 1945–1990* (London: J.M. Dent, 1993) is also supplied, for ease of reference. Similarly, Raymond Garlick's poems are quoted from the original volumes, with their location in his *Collected Poems 1946–86* (Llandysul: Gwasg Gomer, 1987) provided where relevant.

Introduction:
A Corresponding Voice

Jason Walford Davies

I

In an elegy to R.S. Thomas, the Welsh poet Twm Morys imagines an English journalist arriving at Thomas's cottage in the village of Y Rhiw on the Llŷn Peninsula. The poem alludes to the now (in)famous photograph of Thomas as if glowering at the outside world from an ancient doorway. The photograph, by Howard Barlow, accompanied the obituaries of the poet published in *The Times*, *The Independent* and *The Daily Telegraph* on 27 September 2000, and was also used on the cover of Justin Wintle's biography, *Furious Interiors: Wales, R.S. Thomas and God* (1996) – a volume mentioned by Thomas in one of the letters published here. The photograph helps Twm Morys broach the subject of Thomas's personality as it is regularly projected in the press in England, and often in the English-language press in Wales:

> Be' welodd yr hac boliog – o Lundain,
> A landiodd mor dalog?
> Nid brenin ar ei riniog,
> Nid dyn trist, a'i Grist ar grog,
>
> Ond dyn gwyllt, fel dewin o'i go'. – Hyll iawn
> Yw'r lluniau ohono:
> R.S. sych yn ei ddrws o,
> Ac R.S. oer ei groeso.

What did he see, the fat London hack,
  Who turned up so brazenly?
Not a king on his threshold,
Not a sad man, his Christ crucified,

But a wild man, like a mad magus. – Most ugly
  The pictures taken of him:
Dry R.S. at his door,
R.S. of the cold welcome.

A recluse, then – a mad extremist, 'the Ogre of Wales'?[1] Twm
Morys's elegy sensitively redresses the balance:

  R.S. yn oer ei groeso?
  Nid i'r un o'i adar o!
  Carai ei wraig, carai win,
  Carai'r ifanc, a'r rafin,
  A charai holl drwch yr iaith,
  Ei hofarôls, a'i hafiaith . . .[2]

  R.S. cold in his welcome?
  Not to any of his birds!
  He loved his wife, he loved wine,
  He loved the young, and the good-for-nothing,
  And he loved the language's length and breadth,
  Its overalls, and its zest . . .[3]

But, even allowing for poetic licence, one feels like asking in
turn why Twm Morys's journalist has to be a 'hack' and 'fat'.
By the same token, mightn't Morys's favourable view of
Thomas seem itself a little too easy, over-compensating? But
his praising *cywydd* couplets at least make room for the
sensitivity of R.S. Thomas's creative relationship with others
and other things. Like the letters to Raymond Garlick
published here, the poem is a corrective to the knee-jerk view
of him as not only extremely private ('the hermit/ of the rocks'

as he describes himself in one of his finest poems[4]), but also as extremist and antisocial.

II

Whether directly or at a tangent, we reveal ourselves more tellingly in letters than in photographs and more fully in both than in journalistic spins. In the eight years since R.S. Thomas's death, a substantial number of his letters has come to light, but not until now from any really extended correspondence. It is that *extended* commitment to keep in touch for half a century that makes these letters to the poet and critic Raymond Garlick unusual. It was R.S. Thomas himself who, a year before his death, directed me to what he called 'this one unbroken correspondence'. It has the natural appeal of multiple, changing themes, small and large, over a period from June 1951 to December of the last year of the millennium. But these unusually consistent letters do not exist in a vacuum. Before considering them directly, therefore, it is worth drawing attention to two important individual letters sent to two other correspondents of national significance.

First, a revealing letter to the novelist Islwyn Ffowc Elis of 22 September 1952. It is an early expression of the tension that went to the making of Thomas's achievement as a poet. We sense his envy of the younger Ffowc Elis, who had just published his collection of essays, *Cyn Oeri'r Gwaed* ('Before The Blood Grows Cold') – a volume that had won the Prose Medal at the National Eisteddfod the previous year:

> Fel y gwyddoch erbyn hyn Cymraeg a fuasai fy nghyfrwng i pe cawswn fy magu yn iawn, ond yr wy'n gorfod sgrifennu mewn iaith estron oherwydd bod gwell gafael gennyf ynddi. Ond ni fodlonaf ar y sefyllfa tra byddwyf byw. Dyna'r drwg a wnaeth hanes i un fel myfi – holltodd fy mhersonoliaeth.

Da gennyf weld nad yw'r un anhawster yn eich llethu chwi. Cymraeg yw'ch iaith naturiol a Chymraes yw'ch gwraig. Gallwch fyw bywyd normal felly – hyd y caniatâ'r byd abnormal hwn.

Yr ydych yn ddyn ieuanc hefyd – y mae eich bywyd o'ch blaen. Bron nad wyf yn cenfigennu wrthych. Dyn anwybodus ydwyf. Pe bawn innau'n bump ar hugain oed, buaswn yn ceisio gwneud yn well o'm bywyd nad [*sic*] wyf wedi wneud.

Yr ydych yn ddyn addawol. Peidiwch â gwastraffu eich adnoddau. Dyna'r prif berygl i Gymro heddiw. Yn fy marn i, nid yw'r rhan fwyaf o'n cyd-Gymru [*sic*] yn werth bothran â hwy. Os oes arnoch eisiau datblygu eich dawn, ni fedrwch fforddio plesio ffyliaid.[5]

As you know by now, Welsh would have been my medium if I had been raised correctly, but I am forced to write in a foreign language because I have a better grasp of it. But I won't be happy with the situation as long as I live. That is the damage that history has inflicted on one such as myself – it split my personality.

I'm glad to see that the same difficulty does not afflict you. Welsh is your natural language and your wife is Welsh-speaking. You can therefore live a normal life – as far as this abnormal world allows.

You are also a young man – your life is ahead of you. I'm almost jealous of you. I'm not a learned man. If I too were twenty-five years old, I would try to make more of my life than I have.

You are a man of promise. Don't waste your resources. That is the main danger for a Welshman today. In my opinion, the majority of our fellow-Welshmen are not worth bothering with. If you want to develop your talent, you can't afford to please fools.

One of the most interesting aspects of the letter is the forthrightness with which Thomas, at this extremely early stage in his career, offers advice, mentor-like, to Ffowc Elis, at the same time bridging the divide between the two literatures of Wales. Ironically, this forthrightness sits alongside a good deal of its opposite, namely Thomas's lack of confidence in his Welshness, having been, as he saw it, deprived early of his main cultural inheritance, the Welsh language itself. 'Forgive this fatherly letter,' he says, 'I'm approaching forty!'. Elis was not much more than a decade younger;[6] Thomas's word 'tadol' ('fatherly') acknowledges delicately, and punningly, the danger of patronization.

Our second example is a previously unpublished letter of almost exactly forty years later, dated 24 August 1992, to another winner of the National Eisteddfod's Prose Medal, the novelist and short story writer Robin Llywelyn, who had won the prize earlier that month for his novel *Seren Wen ar Gefndir Gwyn* ('A White Star on a White Background'):

> Cefais amser i ddarllen eich llyfr bellach, ac mae'n dda gen i ddweud iddo ddod fel awel iach i'm buwyd [*sic*]. Bûm i'n yr ysbyty'n ddiweddar ac roedd iaith Cymry'r ward yn ddigon i'm digalonni'n llwyr. Ond yna daeth eich llyfr i ddangos mai fel'na y dylai'r werin, neu hyd yn oed y proletariat Cymraeg siarad.
>
> Pan fydda i'n darllen Joyce a Beckett ac awduron tebyg, bydda i'n gofyn i'm fy [*sic*] hun a ydi'n bosibl gwneud hyn yn Gymraeg? Awgryma'ch ffantasi'i bod hi.[7]

> *I have now had time to read your book, and I am pleased to be able to say that it came into my life like a breath of fresh air. I have been in hospital recently and the language of the Welsh-speaking Welshmen on the ward was enough to dishearten me completely. But then your book arrived to show*

that that is how ordinary Welsh-speaking folk, or even the Welsh-speaking proletariat, should talk.

When I read Joyce and Beckett and other similar authors, I ask myself whether it is possible to do this in the Welsh language. Your fantasy suggests that it is.

What compelled Thomas to write to the author of this groundbreaking postmodernist fantasy novel (this time, an author forty-five years his junior) was, in particular, his admiration for the robustness of the work's colloquial Welsh coupled with its verbal inventiveness. (It is interesting to note that the novel occasioned a lively debate as to its accessibility for ordinary readers, given its perceived ludic challenges.[8]) Thomas's congratulatory letter reminds us of his consistent emphasis in his Welsh-language essays on the link between the muscularity of a nation's living language, its speakers' self-respect, and the resourcefulness and relevance of that language as an artistic medium.[9] The letter to Robin Llywelyn also offers a striking counterpoint to Thomas's comment in an interview in 1990: 'I have now reached a position in old age, when the habit of poetic expression in English is so ingrained that I cannot conceive that I could have written so in Welsh. I cannot see how Welsh as it is now would have been available for the requirements I make upon language'.[10]

III

Naturally, in R.S. Thomas's letters to Raymond Garlick we have a correspondence of far more varied range, within roughly the same range of years – from 1951, when Thomas had only a single, slim volume of poetry to his name, to 1999, when illness was closing in on a world-famous poet. They are all in English, apart from one in Welsh of May 1952 written, significantly, after the first personal meeting of the two Welsh-learners at Garlick's home in Argyle Street, Pembroke Dock.

The letter draws on further Welshness in that it records that, on his return journey from Pembroke Dock, Thomas called on '[translation] the old friend D.J. in Fishguard and had an interesting conversation and a welcome from Mrs Williams – and then, on with my journey through Aberystwyth to Manafon' (p. 10). D.J. Williams (1885–1970) was one of the twentieth century's most celebrated Welsh prose writers, an early member of Plaid Genedlaethol Cymru (later Plaid Cymru/The Party of Wales), and one of the three, with Saunders Lewis and Lewis Valentine, imprisoned for their symbolic act of arson in 1936 at the bombing school in Penyberth, Llŷn. R.S. Thomas's move to the parish of Aberdaron in Llŷn, in his career-long search to find a living in a fully Welsh-speaking community, was 15 years away, but the Welsh language of that one letter in 1952 symbolized an embrace that aligned Garlick with those people whom Thomas most deeply admired.[11] It should be added, though, that it took a long time for both to dispense with formal greetings at the opening of letters. 'One of the things I have been meaning to tell you', Thomas wrote in February 1956, 'is to drop the Mr. – Thomas, or Ronald, or R.S. – anything rather than that millstone of age round my neck' (p. 34). In turn, it brings to mind Garlick's comment on himself in his poem 'Personal Statement': 'Mister to most, a formal man/ . . . for me a poem is first a frame',[12] where the sonic sequence *Mst . . . mst . . . frm . . . frm . . . frst . . . fr* is already itself 'first a frame'. But the frames of poetry are one thing, human correspondence something else.

There was in this way and in others, and in the best sense, a ritualistic edge to the correspondence. The letters offer a subtle tracing of the history of Wales and of the 'Anglo-Welsh' condition through the eyes of one of the greatest poets of the second half of the twentieth century, in correspondence with a central figure of Welsh Writing in English as both fine poet and critic, and influential teacher. But to read the letters is to be absorbed most of all into concrete situations. And there is another kind of concreteness: the sensation of handling these letters in manuscript. Garlick himself recognized this many years ago: 'I have', he said, 'a vivid recollection of the morning when among my post on the doormat was another of those distinctive long envelopes bearing my name and address in the characteristic bold hand, and of how when I opened it I was aware – with humility – of being the first to read that magnificent poem "On Hearing a Welshman Speak"'.[13] It is with that same sense of thisness that it is possible to see (a gift to a graphologist) how Thomas's handwriting changes over the course of half a century, from a smooth tidiness in the early years to a dramatic confidence in the years of eminence to an understandably shaky hand at the very end.

In turn, Thomas commented on the impeccable italic script – calligraphy would not be an overstatement – that, by the late 1950s, Garlick had developed for even his most casual letters.[14] Garlick once recorded that 'My grandfather's written English was finely inscribed, out of reverence for the word – the shape as well as the sound of thought'.[15] In a letter of 1956 Thomas wrote, 'I hold your calligraphy up to Gwydion [Thomas's son, then 10 years old] as an example!' (p. 33), and in 1963 wrote, 'I always feel I should frame your calligraphic efforts' (p. 58). As it happens, it was Garlick who was to frame some of Thomas's letters to *him*. They take a natural, honoured place on a wall in his Carmarthen home, side by side with framed letters from writers such as Waldo Williams, Saunders Lewis, John Ormond, John Tripp, Idris Davies and John Cowper Powys. It is an alternative portrait gallery – not of faces but of written words by major writers who were also friends. It adjusts, but to the same honouring end, Ben Jonson's advice at the beginning of the First Folio of Shakespeare, that we should look 'not on his picture, but his book'. In reverse, it is close to the national/personal pride of Yeats's lines in 'The Municipal Gallery Re-visited':

> You that would judge me do not judge alone
> This book or that, come to this hallowed place
> Where my friends' portraits hang and look thereon;
> Ireland's history in their lineaments trace;
> Think where man's glory most begins and ends
> And say my glory was I had such friends.[16]

IV

Before considering other aspects of the correspondence, it is worth noting the use made in the poetry of both writers of the very *genre* of letter writing. It is something at once more precise and more generalizing than the ordinary 'I . . . you' of poetry. Garlick has his 'Letter to London' and his 'Postcard from Delphi'.[17] And in his poem 'Trinities' an incisive sense of humour records that, in Trinity College, Carmarthen he often received mail addressed to Trinity College, Cambridge:

> some English sorter, idle eyed,
> sorts only to the shared CA –
> Carmarthen, Cambridge read the same
> to postal chauvinists at play.[18]

It is the equivalent of Wales's problem of being awash with Joneses. By today, of course, the World Wide Web's solution is that email to Trinity College, Carmarthen, as opposed to that in Cambridge or Dublin or to the hundreds of other Trinities world wide, be delimited as 'trinity-cm'. Obviously a worldly-wise answer. But the 'postal' complaint of Garlick's poem encodes a *cultural* disadvantage, closer to a complaint Thomas made about postal delay. This was in a letter in Welsh in 1948 to the writer and scholar Pennar Davies ('Davies Aberpennar',

1911–96), when Thomas was still a learner of the Welsh language. Postal delay, Thomas wrote, was 'Another example of the fate of Welsh-language letters'.[19] One feels that Thomas – a poet located between two languages, and a natural punster anyway[20] – would have smiled to see his Welsh sentence in translation producing the accidental pun on letters as things sent in the post and 'letters' as a nation's literature. It is appropriate in this context that in Garlick's 'Personal Statement', a poem defining what he sees as the nature and prime purpose of poetry, it is the trope of literal letters that serves his purpose. The poem has to do with Garlick's consistent belief that clarity of mind and expression are crucial: 'communicate,/ or else return to the writer', he says. 'This/ is also poetry's proper fate'. The image of correspondence is developed in the poem's succeeding stanza:

> Sustain it: poetry must cram,
> pack, concentrate, excise, exclude.
> Art aspires to a telegram
>
> of images.[21]

Some fine poet-critics – Anthony Conran, Jeremy Hooker and Tony Bianchi for example – have explored the lines of connection and differences between Thomas's and Garlick's poetry.[22] But it is revealing to attend also to Garlick's prose writing, his autobiographical essays in particular. There, he creatively adumbrates autobiographical facts in R.S. Thomasish terms. For example, it is as Iago Prytherch's kin that Garlick saw the smallholders in the forest of Ommen, his nearest neighbours during his period teaching in the Netherlands between 1961 and 1967: 'Saxon small-farmers, oak-rooted European peasantry with whom Iago Prytherch would find much in common'.[23] And in another autobiographical piece, Garlick defines his problematic relationship with his mother by quoting a strong line from Thomas's poem 'Gifts', in which Thomas deals with his tense relationship with his own mother. 'She had strong views on everything, including her elder son', Garlick writes, then adding, '"From my mother the fear," as R.S. Thomas's poem has it'.[24] It is significant that this one formative influence that Thomas and Garlick share is the subject of two of the most personally telling letters between them (pp. 92 and 93).

But this full complement of Thomas's letters to Garlick now shows the further adaptability of this trope of 'correspondence' in the sense of letters. We now see for the first time how specific Thomas letters are the inspiration behind several of Garlick's most notable poems. Outside the context of the present volume, and given the absence of any explanatory notes, the reader would not know that Thomas was involved at all. Such poems by Garlick reflect his belief in 'Personal Statement' that a poem needs to be as direct and compact as a letter. A Thomas letter is answered by a Garlick poem. 'The Greeting', for example, opens, 'My poor wishes, he wrote: the warm/ Offering of a cold heart'.[25] This is a direct quotation from Thomas's letter to Garlick at Christmas 1977 ('Dear Raymond, Here are my poor Christmas wishes, a warm offering from a cold heart'). Thomas's letter continues, 'A Christian has no right to be despondent, but there is a chill in the air out of the future' (p. 101) – the last eleven words almost in themselves a poem. Garlick's 'The Greeting' continues:

> the warm
> Offering of a cold heart.
> Not so,
> Old friend. Nothing you wish is poor.
> All that you offer us is warm
> With joy and grief, your tenderness
> To life. The vulnerable heart,

By nature and by calling laid
Open to the whole condition
Of poor man, distances itself
Only for one cause: not to be
Overwhelmed. And though the chill draught
Of the anguish of humanity
Sweeps round it, cuts it to the quick,
The thrust of the arterial blood
Is strong and red and hot as theirs.[26]

Even that phrase 'With joy and grief' towards the beginning of the above quotation reminds us of a Thomas poem, 'A Blackbird Singing', where the bird loads its song 'With history's overtones, love, joy/ And grief'.[27] Following this line further we reach, appropriately, another letter – that of Paul to the Galatians: 'But the fruit of the Spirit is love, joy, peace'.[28] A.E. Dyson astutely noticed that Thomas had caused the word 'peace' to crumble into virtually its opposite – 'grief'.[29]

Or take another example: Garlick's poem 'Yours of the 29th' from *A Sense of Time* (1972) – a volume he dedicated, as it happens, to the memory of the poet Waldo Williams who had died the previous year.[30] Garlick's poem opens with the question 'Why Lourdes, not Enlli [Bardsey Island]?'.[31] He is again directly quoting a letter from Thomas, a letter enquiring sensitively about the serious illness (1968–69) of Garlick's son: 'I wonder why it has to be Lourdes. Why not Ynys Enlli?'. Thomas had in 1967 moved to the parish of Aberdaron. Ynys Enlli was part of that parish, only a few miles (but of very treacherous water) from his vicarage. 'In mediaeval times, as you know, three pilgrimages to Enlli equalled one to Rome.' He then wittily hoists the tradition into our own time: 'Now in the jet age, I should reverse the figures . . . [Enlli is] certainly a chancy place to get to' (p. 79). In his poem, Garlick's answer to the question 'Why Lourdes, not Enlli?' is that man needs sometimes to search for God's grace in the turmoil and press of the human world:

> Not Enlli climbing in a cloud
> of light from the green sea,
> Enlli untouched, at peace, and loud
> only with sea-birds' cries;
> but admass Lourdes, light of the crowd,
>
> spring in the concrete drought
> of supermarket, one-way-street,
> asylum, city square.
> Today a man must go to greet
> grace in this wilderness,
> the cool cave in this desert's heat.[32]

A pilgrimage to such a place as Lourdes – which Garlick visited with his family at Easter 1970[33] – was especially instructive not only because of the length of the journey involved but also because of the contrast between its resonance as a place of grace and its commercial vulgarity.

What, in turn, of the image of letter-writing in Thomas's work? An obvious aspect of his polemical prose – and, I would suggest, of his very development as a Welsh-language writer – is the part played from an early stage by that time-honoured thing, a 'letter to the press'. Consider, for example, his letters in Welsh in the period 1946–50 to *Y Llan*, the journal of the Church in Wales, on topics such as the 'Save Europe Fund', 'Leadership', 'The Church and Wales' and 'The Commission',[34] and the consistent letters to the press during the 1970s and 1980s especially.[35] Also relevant are Thomas's numerous letters to the officers of various institutions and causes in his role as Secretary of Cyfeillion Llŷn (The Friends of Llŷn), a pressure group Thomas co-founded in 1985.[36]

Open, public letters, and private letters on public issues, are a characteristic of Garlick's contribution, too – letters Garlick hoped were 'always . . . courteous, but also probing and severe'.[37] They also had the 'functional aims of immediate, lucid communication, information, exposition, and often remonstration' – an activity Garlick described in retrospect as 'a workshop of prose'.[38] And Thomas and Garlick are seen coming together in this epistolary sense when both signed, along with Ned Thomas and Gwyn Williams, an open letter to *The Times* in May 1971, protesting against 'the contemptuous injustice to the Welsh language shown by the courts, the police, and those responsible for non-bilingual road-signs'.[39]

But even more precisely, there is an interesting group of Thomas poems that use, or play on, the actual form of letters. These have a particular resonance in the context of a poet for whom communication (what Garlick calls 'the strident two-way traffic/ of meaningful speech'[40]), or a failure to communicate, were personal themes throughout. I have in mind Thomas poems such as the following: 'A Line from St David's' ('I am sending you this letter,/ . . . I ramble; what I wanted to say/ Was . . .');[41] 'Unposted' ('Dear friend unknown,/ why send me your poems?');[42] 'The Message' ('A message from God/ delivered by a bird/ at my window . . .' – a skilful application in a religious context of the Welsh *cerdd latai* convention of the bird as love-messenger);[43] 'Covenanters: *Paul*' ('Your letters remain/ unanswered, but survive the recipients/ of them');[44] 'Poste Restante' (where the church itself becomes the repository of uncollected messages: 'I want you to know how it was . . . // . . . he would scratch his name and the date/ he could hardly remember, Sunday/ by Sunday');[45] 'The Letter' (1958) ('And to be able to put at the end/ Of the letter Athens, Florence – some name/ That the spirit recalls from earlier journeys . . .// And laying aside the pen, dipped/ Not in tears' volatile liquid/ But in black ink of the heart's well');[46] and a second poem entitled 'The Letter' (1992) ('This morning there came this letter/ from the heart's stranger, promising/ to pray for me. What does that/ mean?').[47] Then, in the posthumous volume *Residues* (2002), there is the poem 'Postcard' ('A notice to inform/ the unlettered: This is Troy . . .').[48] And as for postcards as such – those pregnant missives half-way between telegram and letter – it is worth drawing attention to Thomas's comment, in a recorded presentation of his work, on his poem 'Souillac: Le Sacrifice D'Abraham',[49] that it 'was based . . . not on an actual visit to the French church, but on a reproduction that someone was kind enough to send me as a postcard – proof, if such be needed, of the haphazard and unpredictable way in which poetry can be born'.[50] It is worth adding that the poem 'Postcard' mentioned above was composed in response to a postcard sent to R.S. Thomas by Raymond Garlick from Troy (which Garlick had visited in June 1989). Thomas sent the original typescript of the poem to Garlick, along with a letter in which he actually draws attention to poems prompted by postcards (both now framed on Garlick's wall) (p. 136). It is a nice symmetry: Thomas sends a letter to Garlick, Garlick responds with a poem; Garlick sends Thomas a postcard, Thomas responds with a poem. Nothing better identifies them as corresponding voices.

But the Thomas poem employing most containedly, and therefore most resonantly, the form of a letter is the one pointedly titled 'Correspondence':

> You ask why I don't write.
> But what is there to say?
> The salt current swings in and out
> of the bay, as it has done
> time out of mind. How does that help?

It leaves illegible writing
on the shore. If you were here,
we would quarrel about it.
People file past this seascape
as ignorantly as through a gallery
of great art. I keep searching for meaning.
The waves are a moving staircase
to climb, but in thought only.
The fall from the top is as sheer
as ever. Younger I deemed truth
was to come at beyond the horizon.
Older I stay still and am
as far off as before. These nail-parings
bore you? They explain my silence.
I wish there were as simple
an explanation for the silence of God.[51]

There is here a gradation of correspondences. First, the speaker's unwillingness ('what is there to say?') to fill his letters with polite inconsequentialities is from life: 'He has no small talk' is how one Garlick poem opens, whose title, 'Hermit of the Rocks', reveals Thomas as subject.[52] But 'Correspondence' develops by probing the very concept of reading – not only letters or poems but a world whose manifestations are necessarily not just 'illegible' but ineffable. At the same time, the poem works through *occupatio* – that poetic tease of saying that you cannot do the very thing you then proceed to do. To puzzle about God's silence is partly to read it. It is the only way in which the theme of the *deus absconditus* has any mileage at all. A century earlier, in an age of rigid belief hedged around by disbelief, Gerard Manley Hopkins, too, had used the image of literal, unanswered letters as a metaphor for a deeper absence – not the temporary delay of *poste restante* (a term, as we have seen, Thomas took as the title of one of his best priestly poems), but what, in an equally postal term, Hopkins calls 'dead letters', the *return to sender* of divine silence:

> my lament
> Is cries countless, cries like dead letters sent
> To dearest him that lives alas! away.[53]

But Thomas's 'Correspondence' explores not only the relationship between man and man ('You ask why I don't write') and that between man and God ('the silence of God'), but also that between artist and reader. This last is achieved through a specific literary allusion. 'These nail-parings/ bore you?', Thomas asks his (silent) interlocutor. The image is from James Joyce's *A Portrait of the Artist as a Young Man*: 'The artist, like the God of the creation, remains within, or behind or beyond or above his handiwork, invisible, refined out of existence, indifferent, paring his fingernails'.[54] Hence another reason for Thomas's silence. Further, in the case of the Thomas/Garlick correspondence, apart from a sole surviving letter from Garlick (published here as an appendix), one side is lost to us. The upshot is that we are left to infer and surmise – and only sense the presence of the other side.

V

If we focus more biographically on the way the lives of our two correspondents themselves 'corresponded', other revealing points emerge. Both poets, in a sense, 'discovered' Wales, one from the inside, the other from outside, though even that distinction is only relative in each case. In an autobiographical essay of 1994, Garlick refers to his visits to North Wales as a young boy in the 1930s, and to his journeying to Degannwy by train to visit his grandparents:

After Chester, there was the heightened consciousness of entering Wales, the frequent stops along the northern coast, the sea on the right, hills rising to the left, and – as we neared our destination – a magnificence of mountains.[55]

It is revealing to set Garlick's experience alongside Thomas's, who refers in his radio broadcast 'Y Llwybrau Gynt' ('Former Paths', 1972) to his experience, also in the 1930s, of travelling home to Holyhead from Cardiff on a train, and of his own 'heightened consciousness' on seeing, anew as it were, the land to the west:

the line from Cardiff to Shrewsbury runs along the Marches, with the plains of England on the one side and the hill-country of Wales on the other. I was often stirred on seeing these hills rising in the west. Sometimes night would start to fall before we reached Ludlow. Westwards the sky would be ablaze, reminding one of the battles of the past. Against that radiance the hills rose dark and threatening as if full of armed men waiting for a chance to attack. To the west, therefore, there was a romantic, dangerous, mysterious land.[56]

The poet born in Wales and the one born outside are for a moment parallel, though at no stage interchangeable. They both first set about learning the Welsh language in earnest, and identifying with its culture, at exactly the same time, namely the early 1940s – Thomas in Manafon, with the help of a friend and of Caradar's Welsh-learners' textbooks; and Garlick in evening classes, during the blackout, on the north Wales coast at Llandudno.[57] The Second World War was in both cases, though again in different ways, the catalyst in this finding of a cultural home. 'The war', Garlick writes in his poem 'Notes for an Autobiography', 'Finally opened me the door// Of Wales for a lifetime'.[58]

As a young boy, Garlick had visited North Wales almost every year throughout the 1930s. To reach the beaches of Anglesey it was necessary to travel through Bangor. 'I was always profoundly impressed', he wrote, 'by the sombre splendour of the line of university buildings rising against the sky – not for one moment dreaming that, by the middle of the next decade, I should myself be an undergraduate there'.[59] One of the undergraduates already there at that time (1932–35) was R.S. Thomas, even if he confessed to Garlick in a letter of November 1956 that 'I'm afraid my stay there was little more than a tune hummed thoughtlessly' (p. 41). The pictorial frisson with which Garlick describes 'the sombre splendour of the line of university buildings rising against the sky' is matched in Thomas, but prompted by a scene more completely from the world of nature. During a meeting of clergy in the vicarage of Llanarmon Dyffryn Ceiriog, Denbighshire, towards the end of the 1930s, 'as he [R.S. Thomas] looked through the window, he saw the long spur of Y Berwyn rising against the sky, and a thrill went through him'.[60] Though the image chosen by both poets was in two different languages, Thomas's original phrase in Welsh, 'yn codi yn erbyn yr wybren', cannot translate as anything but Garlick's 'rising against the sky', and of course vice versa. But what is crucial is that this parallel topographical moment was part of a Welsh cultural awakening for both poets. The commitment was bound, naturally, to differ in emphasis between the two. But the striking image – vision even – of raised ground against the sky brings to mind the assertion of a major Welsh-language poet who became an important friend to both. In his sonnet 'Cymru a Chymraeg' ('Wales and the Welsh Language' – not the same thing at all as the more usual 'Wales and the Welsh'), Waldo Williams wrote:

Dyma'r mynyddoedd. Ni fedr ond un iaith eu codi
A'u rhoi yn eu rhyddid yn erbyn wybren cân.[61]

Here are the mountains. Only one language can raise them
And set them in their freedom against a sky of song.

This was a point of view that Thomas cherished and came to represent. It proved a position (almost literally a vantage-point) on Wales that Garlick – more naturally urban, cosmopolitan and international, and a great champion of bilingualism – could not subscribe to. It is a divergence of opinion that is, as one might say, registered in the letters.

VI

It was as a student reading English at Bangor that Raymond Garlick first encountered R.S. Thomas as a writer. And, given the two poets' rich contribution to the genre of the radio poem,[62] it is appropriate that it was a radio programme, a medium that then more than now bridged separation, that brought the two together. Their detailed interest in the form was to continue. In September 1952, three days after Thomas's radio ode for four voices, *The Minister*, had been broadcast, Thomas wrote to Garlick saying that he 'was astonished at the B.B.C.'s rendering of my "pryddest". I thought they read it appallingly . . . The B.B.C. read verse shockingly, I think' (p. 13). Six years earlier, in 1946, Garlick had been invited by the poet and academic Alun Llywelyn-Williams, at the time a producer with BBC radio, to take part in two radio programmes under the title 'Welsh Muse: Our Modern Poets' – two broadcasts that arose from the anthology *Modern Welsh Poetry*, edited by Keidrych Rhys two years earlier.[63] The second programme was broadcast on 21 November 1946, and in the present context it is interesting for two reasons. It featured a very early treatment of Thomas's work by Pennar Davies – a fact the latter recalled with justifiable pride in a 1990 article on Thomas.[64] Secondly, the person invited to read two of the poems chosen to represent Thomas's work – 'Iago Prytherch' ('Ah, Iago, my friend . . .') and 'A Priest to His People' (poems that were to appear before the end of the year in Thomas's first collection, *The Stones of the Field*) – was the young Bangor undergraduate, Raymond Garlick.[65]

R.S. Thomas was five years later to submit his first poem to *Dock Leaves*, the periodical edited by Garlick from 1949 to 1960.[66] In his first letter to Garlick, in June 1951, Thomas expresses the view that in the absence of a range of cultural journals providing a forum for English writing out of, or about, Wales – especially by new voices – 'the Welsh movement' lacked 'what could be a very powerful ally' (p. 3). The poems and reviews he offered to submit to *Dock Leaves*, and the serious critical notice they in due course received, especially in Garlick's influential Editorials, added weight to this new, but already important, periodical. At the same time, from the start, a symbiotic relationship between the two poets was forged. In turn this became the foundation of the letters published here, an exchange of news and ideas that includes personal, intellectual and professional support, and discussions of each other's work – and that of other writers – spanning half a century.

An interesting aspect is the relationship between the correspondence and the forum of *Dock Leaves* itself. Often, exchanges in the letters bear further fruit in Garlick's own contributions to the periodical. For instance, his extended Editorial in the Winter 1955 issue is a treatment of Thomas's *Song at the Year's Turning*, published that year. Garlick confronts the complaint that Thomas, in poems such as 'Welsh Landscape' and 'Welsh History', is too censorious of Wales and the Welsh:

> In connection with this group of poems [the point should be made that] a poem may be born from a mood just as much as from a balanced emotional or intellectual

attitude. It should not be assumed that a point of view which finds relief in a poem or two necessarily represents a sustained conviction on the writer's part.[67]

To this end Garlick has the authority of Thomas's own opinion behind him, relayed from a letter of three years earlier:

> If you are having good discussions about 'gnawing the carcase' etc. I don't see why I should put a stop to them by explaining what I mean! After all, so much poetry is the result of a mood.
>
> However, I should think most 'Anglo-Welshmen' who really know their country are ambivalent towards it.

And it is worth quoting Thomas's remark at the end of this letter. It throws a bright light on his use of a hymn by Pantycelyn at the end of 'Border Blues' – a poem that was to appear the following year in Garlick's *Dock Leaves*.[68]

> I would like to boast that no one loves the old things of Wales more than I do, and yet there is something fearful sometimes in thinking 'ni bydd diwedd byth ar sŵn y delyn aur [there will never be an end to the sound of the golden harp]'. (p. 8)

VII

As already mentioned, there is in this exchange of letters (on one side, only inferable) a lively treatment of each other's verse and of that of other poets. Here again, there is an element of Thomas in the role of mentor (the word, in fact, Garlick used of Thomas in an autobiographical essay in 1995[69]). 'I wish I could have shown so much achievement at your age', Thomas writes in a letter of December 1953 after Garlick had sent him some of his poems. 'It is good to see you striving for an individual means of expression. Wales should be grateful that an Englishman has dug his feet so firmly into the country of his adoption' (p. 19). And a year later: 'I hope you don't think I am patronising or condescending. I happen to be several years older than you and have had to work and try and fail, and am still far from any sort of goal. So when I say your work has promise, you can understand, if you like, that it has far more promise than mine showed at your age' (p. 29).

Thomas was referring to Garlick's volume *The Welsh-Speaking Sea* (1954), whose very title of course was a phrase from Dylan Thomas's 1945 broadcast 'Memories of Christmas', printed in 1946 in *Wales* and posthumously collected in *Quite Early One Morning* in 1954.[70] R.S., quite rightly in some ways, thought Dylan 'a bad influence – a better sign post than map'. He goes on to claim that Dylan Thomas 'wrote some half dozen first class lyrics – the rest is dross' (p. 29),[71] with that last phrase a quotation from Pound's lines, 'What thou lovest well remains,/ the rest is dross', from the *Pisan Cantos*.[72] Thomas is also echoing himself: a year earlier, following Dylan Thomas's death, he had turned down Garlick's invitation to write on Dylan – 'I don't feel I have anything original I can say about Dylan Thomas. I don't fancy myself as a critic I am afraid. He wrote a few major lyrics'. He then added as a doubtfully plausible reason for not contributing, 'I don't feel his work has sufficient facets to lend itself to detailed analysis' (p. 18). It is ironic that R.S. Thomas's poem of the same period, 'Song at the Year's Turning' (first published in the *Times Literary Supplement* on 23 April 1954), was an oblique elegy to his namesake,[73] named after the last lines of Dylan's 'Poem in October': 'O may my heart's truth/ Still be sung/ On this high hill in a year's turning'.[74] Deepening the irony is that the poem 'Song at the Year's Turning' lent its title to the volume that brought R.S. Thomas to national prominence the following year.[75]

Song at the Year's Turning opened with a highly

complimentary Introduction by John Betjeman, a big 'name' who helped Thomas's claim to recognition with the genuine if traditional assertion that 'The "name" which has the honour to introduce this fine poet to a wider public will be forgotten long before that of R.S. Thomas'.[76] The fulsomeness was soon slapped down by the very receiver of its blessing. Garlick in a letter of 1956 had referred to Betjeman's words of praise. In reply, Thomas was concerned to block any wrong impression given of his work:

> Betjeman's remarks to which you refer are almost drivel and are not a true statement of my views at all. To say Yeats influenced me and in the same breath to say I don't believe in reading aloud is rubbish. Neither do I shun the XIX Century as Betjeman says I do. The remark about the inner ear is a poetic platitude. (p. 36)

In fact, Betjeman's remarks are nowhere near drivel. Garlick's letter (a good example of the richness of his side of the correspondence, so sadly missing) had obviously drawn attention to three brief sentences towards the end of Betjeman's Introduction, concerning influence, method and style. Thomas was right to deny that he avoided nineteenth-century English poetry – how *could* he avoid it? – and yet the detail in Betjeman's claim, that Thomas did so 'because he thinks that [its] obvious and jingly rhythms might upset his own sense of metre',[77] suggests Thomas might have once casually said as much (he did, after all, travel to London to meet Betjeman and the volume's publisher, Rupert Hart-Davis[78]). Any possible disapproval on Thomas's part of 'reading aloud' – whether the act is that of the reader, of the poet in the process of composition, or of the poet in a public reading – raises interesting questions. Certainly, Thomas seemed to enjoy, if austerely, the numerous poetry-readings that Betjeman's leg-up in 1955 made possible for almost half a century. Also interesting is Thomas's description of Betjeman's reference to an 'inner ear' as just a 'poetic platitude'. As it happens, thirteen years later – possibly recalling Betjeman's words, and making amends – Thomas publicly stated that 'Yeats used to compose aloud, whereas I compose on the page . . . I believe that the inner ear which goes into operation as the eye runs along a line of poetry is more delicate and subtle than the outer ear'.[79]

Betjeman commented that 'This retiring poet had no wish for an introduction to be written to his poems'.[80] Indeed, the situation of the 'retiring poet' in relation to the older Betjeman is the inverse of Thomas's 'mentor' role in relation to the younger Garlick. In the latter case, Thomas consistently offers advice and encouragement, drawing attention in some cases to individual poems, as in the letter in August 1964 thanking Garlick for a dummy copy of his *Landscapes and Figures*, where Thomas says that his favourite in that volume is 'Penumbra' (p. 62).[81] The choice is significant: there is a striking relationship in terms of theme, atmosphere and treatment between that poem and 'Harvest End', Thomas's nuanced rendering of 'Diwedd y Cynhaeaf' by Caledfryn (William Williams, 1801–69), a translation published over twenty years later in his 1986 volume *Experimenting with an Amen*.[82]

All this makes us realize that this is far from any one-way 'master and pupil' situation. It was advantageous to Thomas, too, to have, in the form of this correspondence, not only the promptings, nudges and challenges, but the expert, sensitive and honest response of another poet who was also a fine scholar and critic. It gave him, in a career that came increasingly to be journalistically under siege, the opportunity to discuss and consider his own work and attitudes constructively. A clear example is a letter of August 1995 dealing with his poem 'Questions to the Prophet', which had appeared three years earlier in *Mass for Hard Times*.[83] 'The poem', Thomas wrote,

> aims to explore the ironies in the Old and New Testament as well as a paradox of Zeno, the Greek philosopher.
>
> Experience of life teaches that hardly any of the verses in the Bible can be taken at face value. Each of these verses should be looked at carefully with the realisation that profound issues are involved.
>
> For instance there is much sentimentality connected with the idea of childhood; yet true adulthood knows things which are beyond a child's grasp.
>
> Similarly there is a lot of condemnation of wealth, and yet it is the secret desire of the majority of mankind.
>
> So with prostitution. It is not a pleasant idea; yet it is practised world-wide and amongst fallen humanity who can compute the profit and loss?
>
> We know that most of Christ's sayings were metaphorical, yet by taking one such as going into the kingdom without one's right hand literally a new twist can be given it. (p. 151)

'Where will the little child lead them/ who has not been there before?', the poem asks; 'With our right hand off, with what/ shall we beg forgiveness in the kingdom?'.[84]

Even more important are those places where Thomas responds, as it were, to Garlick's response to his work. In a letter of October 1966, for example, Thomas thanks Garlick for his extended comments on his volume *Pietà*, which had just been published. It is clear that not all of Garlick's comments were complimentary, and that, in particular, he didn't like the poem for voices, 'Gospel Truth'.[85] The latter point led Thomas to explain that 'The cohering theme is the way God i.e. love works out his purpose even in such weird folk as some of my Montgomery farmers. But evidently I have got lost among the characters, so that the wood is not visible for the trees'. Garlick had been spot-on. '[I]t is good of you to write at such length', Thomas says, 'so much more helpful than the slick and spiteful half truths of the columnists' (p. 66). This was probably a direct reference to one of Thomas's *bêtes noirs*, Professor John Carey, who four months earlier had reviewed *Pietà* in the *New Statesman*, commenting that '[Thomas's] reputation thrives on the misapprehension that to be really real you have to write about muck-heaps and mangel-wurzels, though they are as familiar to most of us as knights in armour. When does a furrow become a rut?'.[86]

That rhetorical question, patently ungenerous, connects nevertheless with what is most revealing in Thomas's 1966 letter on the subject of *Pietà*, namely his thoughts about the personal struggle involved in sustaining poetic power:

> the older I get, the less sure I feel. Loss of nerve? 'The writer's middle years' as [Lawrence] Durrell calls them? A lyric poet soon loses his shine I fear and there is the awful struggle to 'concoct the old heroic bang' as Hughes puts it. You know as a poet how some poems go cold on one – a distressing feeling – and I'm afraid more poems in Pietà have done this than in any other book. (p. 66)

The phrase 'concoct the old heroic bang' is from Ted Hughes's poem 'Famous Poet',[87] and is particularly interesting in the light of the key role that Hughes's poetry – his volume *Crow* (1970) in particular – was soon to play in Thomas's work as a kick-start to a new phase from the early 1970s, or the volume *H'm*, onwards.[88] In a letter of April 1978 Thomas described Ted Hughes as 'my favourite reader of poetry' (p. 103) – not least, perhaps, as an antidote to the efforts of BBC actors.

However, Thomas's 1966 letter had closed on a note of lost power:

> I have said some sharp things about the English and the urban outlook, so must expect to be attacked. The trouble is in thinking one is important enough to be attacked. It is more likely that the work is after all just bad. (p. 66)

It is a subject that surfaces more than once during the correspondence. The letters are those of a major poet thought of generally as anything but mealy-mouthed, who was regarded rather as polemically confident in his attitudes. But they yield glimpses of a poet genuinely uncertain of the nature, quality and status of his contribution. Confidence and uncertainty are always there in tension, sometimes in the very tone of quite ordinary pronouncements. A letter of December 1997, before any final illness had set in, opens with the sad remark, 'I soldier on with an uneasy feeling of having outstayed my welcome', and towards the end repines that 'the lyrical spring is running dry at last. I was lucky it ran for so long' (p. 156) – this, it should be noted, over thirty years after his misgivings about *Pietà*, just quoted. But the central letter in this context is one sent two days before Thomas's 70th birthday in 1983, where he measures himself against Rimbaud, Valéry, Yeats and Eliot: 'There is certainly no feeling of achievement at all, but rather of a falling short of what I would have wished to achieve. The sort of yard-sticks I have used have been Bateau Ivre, Le Cimetière Marin, Sailing to Byzantium, Gerontion etc. And when one falls short of those, one knows one hasn't been chosen' (p. 116). Five years earlier, urging Garlick to read Geoffrey Hill's *Tenebrae* (1978), Thomas had said that Hill was 'a fine poet, certainly the best now writing in English. I wish I wrote with his economy and intelligence. And he is only 46, so there must be much good work to come' (p. 110). It is key details such as these that form the background against which we should read one of Thomas's last poems, 'Gravestone', from the posthumously published volume *Residues*:

> I fell with my poem
> nearly there. So many times
> I did this, hurting my pride
> more than my pocket. Patient
>
> earth, building your house
> with our bones, keep these pieces
> of me that in better
> poets my pride may be mended.[89]

VIII

More epistolary than apostolic, ordinary details too help form the background against which poems stand. Relishing the detail thrown up in the hubbub of literary letter-writing in the seventeenth century, Virginia Woolf once said that 'the bare landscape becomes full of stir and quiver and we can fill in the spaces between the great books with the voices of people talking'.[90] Authentic in the same way in Thomas's letters are those small biographical details here and there that allow us to glimpse in the course of the daily life of a major poet those things that fill in 'the spaces between the great books'. The letter, for example, where Thomas asks Garlick for details of the times and prices of the ferries from Pembroke Dock to Cork to compare with those from Holyhead to Dublin, his dry humour coming through even in being at a loss: 'I haven't a clue as to whom to write for information. I foresee a letter addressed to British + Irish Steampacket Co., Pembroke Dock, as likely to return to sender' (p. 102). He was planning in the main a bird-watching visit to Cape Clear in County Cork (a previous visit, a decade earlier, had resulted in the poem

'Shrine at Cape Clear'[91]). Or those darker comments, as when Thomas deplores the fact that the authorities were blocking his letters of ordinary thanks to John Jenkins, the imprisoned Welsh political activist, who had sent Thomas Christmas cards (pp. 90 and 95); or when he records that 'I was in Luxor two days before the massacre' in 1997 (p. 156); or the letters recording his deep disappointment regarding (as he saw it) the lack in the Llŷn Peninsula of an active Welsh political consciousness – a disappointment deepened by the fact that the search for such a communal consciouness had been one of his prime motives for moving there, to his final parish (pp. 70 and 77); or the letters referring to his untiring attempts to support the Welsh language in Llŷn, revealing his absolute commitment, but again not without his characteristic wryness:

> I managed to get the Post Office to put up 'Y Llythyrdy' [The Post Office] which my wife painted, but others, such as the butcher, just laugh uncomfortably at the suggestion that High Class Family Butcher looks a bit odd in Aberdaron. I suppose he thinks visitors confronted by a window full of sheep's carcases might not know what it was if it had Cigydd [Butcher] printed on top. (p. 77)

Indeed, other quotidian experiences are part of major matrices in Thomas's poetry and prose. Take, for example, the epiphany in November 1978 when he

> turned aside to Llanpumsaint in an attempt to look at the East window Elsie [his wife, the artist Mildred E. Eldridge] did years ago. The church was locked, I failed to get an answer at any of the hideous houses, it was like a village of the dead. Then suddenly a herd of cows appeared with four men and dogs. The cows stampeded, the dogs barked, the men shouted in Welsh and a resurrection of a sort occurred. (p. 109)

This is the type of momentary experience – it *can* be only for a moment – that had produced the concept of Abercuawg, the ideal of a Welsh-speaking, rural village or town that is the paradigmatic – and unrealisable – cultural space which makes the modern, contingent world tolerable.[92] So fully did the idea of an ideal village inform Thomas's mind from the beginning in the above letter that the word 'village' dislodged 'visit' in its opening sentence: 'Just a word of thanks for your hospitality during my brief but pleasant village [*sic*]'. The mistake, in its conflation of time and place, captures exactly the nature of Abercuawg; indeed, 'my brief but pleasant village' would be a quintessential description of it. A different but equally powerful example comes in a letter of 31 December 1953:

> Gwydion [the poet's son] is home now. We have just endured a pantomime for him. We go all the way to Shrewsbury to imbibe three hours of English proletarian culture.
> However as there is no Welsh culture to put in its place – there it is. (p. 20)

This leads back, in fuller costume as it were, to the lines in a major Thomas poem, 'Border Blues', which had appeared in Garlick's *Dock Leaves* the previous summer:

> *Eryr Pengwern, penngarn llwyt heno . . .*
> We still come in by the Welsh gate, but it's a long way
> To Shrewsbury now from the Welsh border.
> There's the train, of course, but I like the 'buses;
> We go each Christmas to the pantomime:
> It was Babes in the Wood this year, all about nature.[93]

Garlick's complaint, in one of his *Dock Leaves* Editorials, about *Dylan Thomas: Letters to Vernon Watkins* (1957) is relevant here – that in that volume 'No clue is given to the point of departure – in the poet's inner or outer experience – of the poems'.[94] In contrast, the Thomas-Garlick letters are often about those very points of departure, rather than being any detailed commentary on each other's poems. Garlick never sent Thomas his poems for comment. Those which Thomas encountered – including ones about himself, such as 'Hermit of the Rocks', already mentioned, together with 'Apologia'[95] and the relevantly-titled 'Postcard from Delphi'[96] – he encountered when they were already out there in print. Similarly, any poems Thomas sent to Garlick were not for comment but for interest or consideration for publication. The fact that the friendship was not of the Dylan-Vernon Watkins kind made it in a sense more relaxed and less hectic.

IX

Even so, this was no sedate exchange. There was some very straight talking. It is now clear that Garlick was responsible for 'firming up' (his phrase to the present editor) some of Thomas's views on such aspects as republicanism and pacifism, and that he had on occasion clearly ventured to take Thomas to task about one thing or another. Similarly, the firm stand-off regarding the proportion of early-Thomas-poems-to-late to be included in Raymond Garlick and Roland Mathias's anthology *Anglo-Welsh Poetry 1480–1980* (1984) (p. 119).[97] But a natural sense of drama came, in any case, from the openness of the letters not only to public, controversial aspects of politics and religion, but also to aspects of personal identity and private life. At many points, the public and the personal came together – for instance in Thomas's consistent concern regarding his Church's liturgy. 'I am retiring at Easter', he writes in 1977:

> I shall be 65. I could stay till 70, but I am glad to go from a Church I no longer believe in, sycophantic to the queen, iconoclastic with language, changing for the sake of

change and regardless of beauty. The Christian structure is a meaningful structure, but in the hands of theologians or the common people it is a poor thing. (p. 101)

These are observations that would have had a direct personal resonance for Garlick, whose own loss of faith at this time also involved questions of language and idiom. For Garlick, modernisation of the Roman Catholic Church involved specifically a retreat from the Latin that had been so attractive to the poet in him. As he put it later, describing his successive attachments to three major bodies of worship: 'My conversion . . . was in fact to the stately language of Cranmer, as it would be a few years later to that of the Quaker mystics, and later still to the sublime Latin liturgy. Since all these modes of language assumed the existence of a deity, I took this for granted too. Only very much later in life did the realization dawn that they were in fact art forms, and that so far as their point of reference was concerned my position had not been belief but make-believe'.[98]

Thomas's Christmas letter of 1979 is irradiated by multiple concerns. It had been the year of the massively lost vote on political devolution for Wales, but the letter speaks of a 'malaise', a 'nervous reaction' also personally endemic:

Whenever I am unwell I fall to questioning various postures and tenets too easily and arrogantly held when one is well, both in one's life and in poetry. I am writing like this to you because of the difficulty both of us are having with our allegiance to a church which seems to be abandoning too lightly the wonderful traditions which have sustained over the centuries. (p. 111)

And yet, this is how the letter closes: 'The church is imperfect, God knows, but it has the scriptures and sacraments, if it only will have the grace to let those who prefer the old forms continue to enjoy them. So I shall still go along on Christmas morning. Perhaps you will? Cofion cu [Affectionate regards], Ronald' (p. 111).

X

It is not to equate literary history with religion to say that this sense of breakage and endangered identity is cognate with Thomas's perception of the nature and role of Anglo-Welsh literature and of Anglo-Welshness generally. This was an area in which Thomas and Garlick didn't see eye to eye ('A disagreement between friends' is how Garlick describes it in a short article on the correspondence[99]). In his 1977 lecture 'Hunanladdiad y Llenor' ('The Creative Writer's Suicide'), Thomas went so far as to say that 'if the Anglo-Welsh writer is honest with himself, he will have to admit that it is in a foreign language that he writes'.[100] Even though he had since early adulthood thought of Wales as home, Garlick, the European, could more comfortably see the English language as 'another dress,/ A second weave to Welshness'[101] (a suitably integrating metaphor when we recall the use of 'weave' in the work of the medieval Welsh poets as a trope for the crafted complexity of their art). 'Despite our speech we are not English,/ . . . We are not English', we read at the end of Thomas's 'Border Blues',[102] which Garlick, as we have seen, published in *Dock Leaves* in 1953. But, in what is a highly ventriloquial poem, those words are put into the mouth of a tavern reveller; so we must remember that Thomas's attitude to the boast is likely to be ambivalent. In his critical writings, Garlick on the other hand employs the boast positively, in witness to what he sees as the tradition, since the late fifteenth century, of an authentic 'Anglo-Welsh' literature that isn't just 'English' – in exploration of which Garlick is a central scholar-critic.[103] For the major part of the period of these letters, the phrase 'Anglo-Welsh' was the customary term. Thomas was uneasy about the very label: 'the Anglo-Welsh, as they are called – for the sake of convenience only, remember'.[104] Even so, 'Anglo-Welsh' had the advantage of holding, even visually within the phrase, a tension that is lost in what has become its rather anodyne, if more embracing, replacement – 'Welsh Writing in English'. Thomas's resistance to an unevadable duality was, in his own person, a source of creative tension. But his view hardened over the years, in proportion to his own increasing (to coin a phrase) Welsh-languageness. In a letter of 1971 he wrote that 'There seems something schizophrenic about Wales and its language being saved by the English language' (p. 83). Three years earlier he had told Garlick that

> I'm afraid I can't think like you about bilingualism, although I realise that rationally speaking one tends to get outargued. It depends rather in what part of Wales one lives, I suppose. I can see that the bois bach in the south are in a bit of a jam, as, of course, I am, too, in having to write in English. (p. 71)

Behind the lightness of the phrase 'in a bit of a jam' stands the anguish, the angst, that as good as determined the whole direction of Thomas's career. 'I wish they were in Welsh', he lamented to Garlick regarding the poems in his collection *Later Poems 1972–1982* (1983). And it was significantly in untranslated Welsh that he remarked bitterly, 'Yr hen Saesneg diawledig yn yr isymwybod'. He was telling Garlick of his habit – on sleepless nights, when trying to get back to sleep – of mentally composing highly-wrought strict-metre poems in Welsh (*englynion*), and failing to complete them (p. 115). His explanation for the failure translates as 'The old infernal English in the subconscious'. It reminds us of Idris Davies saying, in one of his poems in Welsh, that 'the verb refuses to play' ('Mae'r ferf yn methu chwareu').[105]

It is also interesting that Thomas often speaks of this anguish in bodily terms – as of a wound, a scar, a pain or a breaking heart. And it is appropriate that one of the most dramatic examples occurs in a poem of tribute to Raymond Garlick himself. Early on in the period of the correspondence, in the 1955 poem 'Commission: *for Raymond Garlick*', published in *Dock Leaves*, Garlick is greeted with the challenge:

> You know our grievance, know the bitter poison,
> Black as despair, seeping from the wound
> Your country dealt us; plead our rightful case
> To those who come to us for what we give,
> Who take and leave us ruined by their taking,
> Since we must give in ways they understand.

The poem closes with the line, 'Open their eyes, show them the heart that's breaking'.[106] The cultural disability as a writer that Thomas kept exploring connects through metaphor with the actual physical disability that is one of Garlick's themes. 'I live in a rakish body framed/ about a spine like a buckled spire// or twisted spring, my uncurled crown of thorn', Garlick writes in 'Biographical Note', a poem Thomas praises in these letters (p. 29). It is a condition that Garlick, in arresting lines, sets in profound relationship to the creativeness of the very act of writing:

> And thus I am, and thus you see me now:
> a hustings for a heart wrapped in a wrack
> lusting for words to shape itself anew.[107]

That half-rhyme on 'now' and 'anew' dramatizes their meaning, counterpointing present fact with the renewal that is one of art's benefits. In a 1969 volume of poetry by John Wain that took the interesting form of *Letters to Five Artists*, one of the 'letters' is to Elizabeth Jennings, a poet transcending personal difficulties. Wain's poem ends:

> Art finishes what action has begun,
>
> But only if its metaphors are true.
> I see your colours and I catch my breath . . .
>
> Your art will save your life, Elizabeth.[108]

It is this firm belief in the reconstituting power of words and imaginative craft that emerges also in Garlick's seminal *Introduction to Anglo-Welsh Literature* (1970) and in the Introduction to the anthology *Anglo-Welsh Poetry 1480–1980*, co-edited with Roland Mathias in 1984. The merging of artistic and personal striving in the line 'lusting for words to shape itself anew' matches, despite differences, the prime cultural yearning in Thomas: '[Those poems,] I wish they were in Welsh'.[109]

XI

In ending, it is appropriate to recall Twm Morys's elegy for Thomas, with which we started. In particular there was that emphasis on the gentle, private side, well known to anyone who knew R.S. Thomas himself at all well. Thomas approached occasions of personal pain and loss in others' lives with sensitivity, no less profound because quietly stated, just as on the other hand there is here a forthright honesty, bluntness even, when he writes about the death of his own mother. At the same time, there is a good helping of good humour, caught perfectly in Twm Morys's cheeky use of the English word 'overalls' in a wonderfully embracing moment in modern Welsh poetry:

A charai holl drwch yr iaith,
Ei hofarôls, a'i hafiaith . . .

And he loved the language's length and breadth,
Its overalls, and its zest . . .

Journalistic snapshots and soundbites just didn't have the extended exposure necessary to catch this side of Thomas. His unflinching criticism of Welsh people's lack of backbone in the face of the erosion of the language and of cultural rights, or what he saw as the puny attractions of the Anglo-American culture that so speciously camouflages these things in tourist Wales, had a sharpness reminiscent of Siôn Cent, the fifteenth-century Welsh poet whose work Thomas admired intensely.

But, then, his criticism holds Wales herself responsible. Side by side in a uniquely extended correspondence such as this there is the helpful wryness of Thomas's sense of humour. In 1971 Garlick's son, wife and sister-in-law were all arrested for protests in the cause of the Welsh language. 'I'm sorry you are in trouble with the police', Thomas wrote in August that year. 'You should live in Llŷn, where [the police] are all too busy being traffic wardens to have time for conspirators against the throne' (p. 84). That the humour, while making inroads, isn't meant to demolish completely the way forward is shown in a letter of December 1992. Here is the laureate of the 'absent God' describing a visit to Greece: 'we pursued God up Olympos, but he vanished, as always, into thin air . . . We did have one downpour on Olympos. Perhaps God is a monkey after all. They like to urinate at strangers' (p. 145). It is only a poet, concerned with the differences that even small words make, who would have opted for urinating *at*, rather than *on*. The same humour works against recalcitrant facts even where they affect, not (as on Olympos) cosmic belief, but private dignity. Thomas is good, for example, on the subject of old age. In sending Garlick bright news in a letter of November 1996, he wrote like this: 'I re-married in August someone I have known for many years, so here we are, two octogenarians trying to ignore the fact' (p. 153).

XII

That only Thomas's letters survive – apart from the one letter from Garlick – is a serious pity. It is a one-sidedness unfortunately true of many important exchanges. But absent answers, because at one time solidly there, remain a presence. Earlier, I evoked Gerard Manley Hopkins's use of the negative phenomenon of 'dead letters' – that is, totally unanswered letters. Here, instead, we as readers play a creative part, imagining the signals and promptings of letters absent on the other side. It is like the resonance – the electric 'frequency' – at work in the poetic form of the 'dramatic monologue' perfected by that other Victorian poet, Robert Browning. It makes the person addressed vivid even when he or she is given no words. That is why the last word can still go to Garlick himself. It is a nice coincidence that fifty years ago, in his Editorial review in *Dock Leaves* of *Dylan Thomas: Letters to Vernon Watkins*, Raymond Garlick mentioned the effect of those particular Browning poems. His words help us focus not only an aspect of the interest of these letters but (though Garlick himself would not wish it) the real tribute they bear to Raymond Garlick himself:

> For one reader, at least, much of the attraction of these letters lies in their oblique revelation (as in a Browning poem) of the character of [the silent] correspondent – generous, patient, fastidious, committed, reticent.[110]

Notes

1 Regarding the latter term, see Byron Rogers, 'Prisoner of the English Tongue', *The Sunday Telegraph Review*, 30 July 1995, 2. In the article Thomas is quoted as saying, 'When they decide you are an ogre, they find the right photograph'; ibid., 1.

2 Twm Morys, 'R.S.', *2* ([Abertawe]: Cyhoeddiadau Barddas, 2002), 30.

3 The translations from the Welsh in the Introduction are my own.

4 R.S. Thomas, 'Sea-watching', *Laboratories of the Spirit* (London: Macmillan, 1975), 64; R.S. Thomas, *Collected Poems 1945–1990* (London: J.M. Dent, 1993), 306.

5 Quoted in T. Robin Chapman's biography of Elis, *Rhywfaint o Anfarwoldeb: Bywgraffiad Islwyn Ffowc Elis* (Llandysul: Gwasg Gomer, 2003), 71.

6 In 1952 Elis was, in fact, 28, not 25.

7 I am grateful to Robin Llywelyn for permission to quote Thomas's letter.

8 On this debate, see Angharad Price, *Rhwng Gwyn a Du: Agweddau ar Ryddiaith Gymraeg y 1990au* (Caerdydd: Gwasg Prifysgol Cymru, 2002), 1–16.

9 See in particular his essay 'Arwahanrwydd Cenedl ac Ansawdd ei Hiaith' ('A Nation's Individuality and the Nature of Its Language'), *Taliesin*, 65 (1988), 88–90.

10 Ned Thomas and John Barnie, 'Probings: An Interview With R.S. Thomas', in William V. Davis (ed.), *Miraculous Simplicity: Essays on R.S. Thomas* (Fayetteville: University of Arkansas Press, 1993), 42.

11 On Garlick's friendship with D.J. Williams, see 'Portfolio', *Planet*, 107 (October/November 1994), 71–72.

12 Raymond Garlick, *A Sense of Europe: Collected Poems 1954–1968* (Llandysul: Gwasg Gomer, 1968), 104; Raymond Garlick, *Collected Poems 1946–86* (Llandysul: Gwasg Gomer, 1987), 17.

13 Raymond Garlick, 'On The Growing of Dock Leaves', *Planet*, 9 (December 1971/January 1972), 73. 'On Hearing a Welshman Speak' was first published in *Dock Leaves*, 5, 14 (Summer 1954), 3. It was chosen by Raymond Garlick as his contribution to Owen Burt and Christine Jones (eds.), *Voices at the Door: An Anthology of Favourite Poems* (Cardiff: University of Wales Press/Shelter Cymru, 1995), 86–87, where it is described by him as 'a quintessentially Anglo-Welsh poem, celebrating in one of the languages of Wales the life of the other'. See also Garlick's comments on the poem in his Editorial, *The Anglo-Welsh Review*, 9, 24, p. 5.

14 See Don Dale-Jones, *Raymond Garlick* (Cardiff: University of Wales Press, 1996), 27.

15 Raymond Garlick, 'The Words in My Life – Passages from an Autobiography', *The Anglo-Welsh Review*, 13, 31 (Summer 1963), 15. Also relevant is Garlick's description of Tŷ'r Mynydd, Brenda Chamberlain's cottage at Rachub, near Llanllechid, where he lived for three years at the end of the 1940s after Chamberlain's move to Bardsey Island: 'On the great beam

1

of the *simne fawr* John Petts had carved – in superb Roman capitals – the words "Boed tangnefedd yn y tŷ hwn" ["Let there be peace in this house"] (the point of departure of my own lifelong preoccupation with fine lettering)'; 'Some Painters', *Planet*, 108 (December 1994/January 1995), 68.

16 Daniel Albright (ed.), *W.B. Yeats: The Poems* (London: J.M. Dent, 1990), 368.

17 Raymond Garlick, *The Welsh-Speaking Sea: Selected Poems 1949–1954* (Pembroke Dock: Dock Leaves Press, 1954), 23; Raymond Garlick, *Travel Notes: New Poems* (Llandysul: Gwasg Gomer, 1992), 19.

18 Raymond Garlick, *Incense: Poems 1972–1975* (Llandysul: Gwasg Gomer, 1976), 16; Garlick, *Collected Poems*, 104.

19 'Beth a ydych yn ei feddwl amdanaf, tybed, am beidio ag ateb eich llythyr gyda throad y post? Ond y gwir yw mai heddiw y cyrhaeddodd ef! Enghraifft arall o dynged y llythyrau Cymraeg' ('What do you think of me, I wonder, for not having answered your letter by return of post? But the truth is that it was only today that it arrived! Another example of the fate of Welsh-language letters'); copy of a letter dated 20 November 1948 in the archives of the R.S. Thomas Study Centre, Bangor University.

20 On Thomas's puns see Damian Walford Davies, '"Double-entry Poetics": R.S. Thomas – Punster', in Damian Walford Davies (ed.), *Echoes to the Amen: Essays After R.S. Thomas* (Cardiff: University of Wales Press, 2003), 149–82.

21 Garlick, *A Sense of Europe*, 104; Garlick, *Collected Poems*, 17.

22 See, for example, Anthony Conran, review of *Incense*, *Poetry Wales*, 12, 3 (1977), 88–90 (the review was republished as 'Raymond Garlick: The Poetry of Anglo-Welsh Opinion' in Conran's *The Cost of Strangeness: Essays on the English Poets of Wales* (Llandysul: Gomer Press, 1982), 307–15); Anthony Conran, 'An Abdication from Time: An Essay on the Collected Poems of Raymond Garlick', *The New Welsh Review*, 1, 1 (Summer 1988), 51 (the essay was republished, with additions, in Conran's *Frontiers in Anglo-Welsh Poetry* (Cardiff: University of Wales Press, 1997), 249–58); Jeremy Hooker, review of *A Sense of Time*, *Poetry Wales*, 8, 4 (1973), 93; Tony Bianchi, 'Let the Poem Shout Praise' (review of *Incense*), *Planet*, 40 (November 1977), 25.

23 See Garlick's essay in Meic Stephens (ed.), *Artists in Wales 2* (Llandysul: Gomer Press, 1973), 91–92.

24 Raymond Garlick, 'A Small Boy in the Thirties – 3', *Planet*, 104 (April/May 1994), 78. Thomas's poem appeared in *Pietà* (London: Hart-Davis, 1966), 17; Thomas, *Collected Poems*, 161.

25 Garlick, *Collected Poems*, 47.

26 Ibid.

27 R.S. Thomas, *Poetry for Supper* (London: Hart-Davis, 1958), 33; Thomas, *Collected Poems*, 85.

28 Galatians 5:22.

29 A.E. Dyson, *Yeats, Eliot and R.S. Thomas: Riding the Echo* (London: Macmillan, 1981), 298.

30 On Garlick's friendship with Waldo Williams, see 'Portfolio', *Planet*, 107 (October/November 1994), 72.

31 Raymond Garlick, *A Sense of Time: Poems and Antipoems 1969–1972* (Llandysul: Gwasg Gomer, 1972), 81.

32 Ibid.

33 See Stephens (ed.), *Artists in Wales 2*, 95.

34 R.S. Thomas, 'Cronfa Achub Ewrop', *Y Llan*, 27 September 1946, 6; 'Arweinyddiaeth', ibid., 7 March 1947, 6; 'Yr Eglwys a Chymru', ibid., 2 September 1949, 5; 'Y Comisiwn', ibid., 3 February 1950, 8.

35 For Thomas's relevant publications during this period, see the bibliographies in Tony Brown and Bedwyr Lewis Jones (eds.), *R.S. Thomas: Pe Medrwn Yr Iaith ac Ysgrifau Eraill* (Abertawe: Christopher Davies, 1988), and Sandra Anstey (ed.), *R.S. Thomas: Selected Prose* (Bridgend: [third edition] Seren, 1995).

36 On Thomas's work on behalf of Cyfeillion Llŷn, see Jason Walford Davies, *Gororau'r Iaith: R.S. Thomas a'r Traddodiad Llenyddol Cymraeg* (Caerdydd: Gwasg Prifysgol Cymru, 2003), 2–3, 19 n.7, and Tony Brown, *R.S. Thomas* (Cardiff: University of Wales Press, 2006), 93–94.

37 Raymond Garlick, 'Inspiration and Perspiration', *Poetry Wales*, 24, 1 (1988), 37.

38 Ibid.

39 'Defenders of Welsh', *The Times*, 28 May 1971, 17. Garlick refers to the letter in his essay in Stephens (ed.), *Artists in Wales 2*, 96–97, where he notes: 'Since then I have been several times assured, with what truth I do not know, that writings of mine have been submitted to the Director of Public Prosecutions. However aberrant a misreading this might imply, only one formed by a civilization which regards language as important could be capable of so moving a tribute to the written word. But I cannot seriously suppose anything I have written, viewed in context, to be worthy of critical interest of this order. Whatever the truth of the matter, the themes of compassion, justice and the restraint of violence have had two more certain consequences: the purging of a too indulgent aestheticism from poetry, and the provision of an impetus to struggle with certain forms of prose' (p. 97).

40 Garlick, *A Sense of Europe*, 103 ('In The National Museum').

41 R.S. Thomas, *The Bread of Truth* (London: Hart-Davis, 1963), 7; Thomas, *Collected Poems*, 123.

42 R.S. Thomas, *Experimenting with an Amen* (London: Macmillan, 1986), 50; Thomas, *Collected Poems*, 514.

43 R.S. Thomas, *Destinations* (Shipston-on-Stour: Celandine Press, 1985), 7; Thomas, *Experimenting with an Amen*, 56; Thomas, *Collected Poems*, 449.

44 R.S. Thomas, *Later Poems 1972–1982* (London: Macmillan, 1983), 173; Thomas, *Collected Poems*, 406.

45 Thomas, *Laboratories of the Spirit*, 13–14; Thomas, *Collected Poems*, 272.

46 Thomas, *Poetry for Supper*, 26.

47 R.S. Thomas, *Mass for Hard Times* (Newcastle upon Tyne: Bloodaxe Books, 1992), 77.

48 R.S. Thomas, *Residues*, ed. M. Wynn Thomas (Tarset: Bloodaxe Books, 2002), 48.

[49] Thomas, *The Bread of Truth*, 43; Thomas, *Collected Poems*, 147.

[50] *The Critical Forum: R.S. Thomas Discusses His Poetry*, Norwich Tapes, 1980.

[51] R.S. Thomas, *Between Here and Now* (London: Macmillan, 1981), 85; Thomas, *Collected Poems*, 378.

[52] Garlick, *Collected Poems*, 46. The poem is entitled 'Poet' in *A Sense of Europe*, 83.

[53] 'I wake and feel the fell of dark'; Catherine Phillips (ed.), *Gerard Manley Hopkins: A Critical Edition of the Major Works* (Oxford: Oxford University Press, 1986), 166.

[54] James Joyce, *A Portrait of the Artist as a Young Man*, ed. Seamus Deane (Harmondsworth: Penguin, 1992), 233.

[55] Garlick, 'A Small Boy in the Thirties – 3', 75.

[56] Jason Walford Davies (ed. and trans.), *R.S. Thomas: Autobiographies* (London: J.M. Dent, 1997), 10.

[57] See ibid., 55, and Garlick, 'A Small Boy in the Thirties – 3', 77.

[58] Garlick, *Collected Poems*, 155. After the outbreak of war, Garlick was sent from London to live with his father's cousin and her husband, who had a business in Degannwy; see Dale-Jones, *Raymond Garlick*, 12, and Garlick's three-part memoir, 'One Boy's War', *Planet*, 151 (February/March 2002), 25–31; 152 (April/May 2002), 52–57; 153 (June/July 2002), 79–85. On Thomas and the Second World War, see M. Wynn Thomas, 'R.S. Thomas: War Poet', *Welsh Writing in English: A Yearbook of Critical Essays*, 2 (1996), 82–97.

[59] Garlick, 'A Small Boy in the Thirties – 3', 77.

[60] Davies (ed. and trans.), *Autobiographies*, 43.

[61] Waldo Williams, *Dail Pren* (Aberystwyth: Gwasg Aberystwyth, 1956), 100.

[62] See, for example, Thomas's *The Minister* (Newtown: Montgomeryshire Printing Co., 1953) (Thomas, *Collected Poems*, 42–55), and the following poems by Garlick: *Requiem for a Poet* (Pembroke Dock: Dock Leaves Press, [1953] (Dock Leaves Pamphlet No. 1)); *Blaenau Observed: A Broadcast Poem* (Pembroke Dock: Dock Leaves Press, 1957); 'Acclamation', *A Sense of Time*, 57–71; 'Fanfare for Europe', *Incense*, 11–13. See also Rhian Reynolds, 'Poetry for the Air: *The Minister*, *Sŵn y Gwynt sy'n Chwythu* and *The Dream of Jake Hopkins* as Radio Odes', *Welsh Writing in English*, 7 (2001–02), 78–105, and Garlick's review of Thomas's *The Minister* in *Dock Leaves*, 4, 11 (Summer 1953), 54–57.

[63] Keidrych Rhys (ed.), *Modern Welsh Poetry* (London: Faber and Faber, 1944).

[64] Pennar Davies, 'Yr Ymchwiliwr Crefyddol', in M. Wynn Thomas (ed.), *R.S. Thomas: Y Cawr Awenydd* (Llandysul: Gwasg Gomer, 1990), 114.

[65] Raymond Garlick discusses his involvement with the two broadcasts in '1944–50: Dock Leaves and Nettles', *The New Welsh Review*, 34, IX:2 (Autumn 1996), 37–40. See also his comments in Stephens (ed.), *Artists in Wales 2*, 87.

[66] Thomas's poem, 'Depopulation of the Hills', appeared in *Dock Leaves*, 2, 6 (Michaelmas 1951), 23.

[67] Raymond Garlick, Editorial, *Dock Leaves*, 6, 18 (Winter 1955), 8.

68 *Dock Leaves*, 4, 11 (Summer 1953), 8–11.

69 Raymond Garlick, 'Dylan Thomas and Others', *Planet*, 109 (February/March 1995), 81.

70 Dylan Thomas, 'Memories of Christmas', *Wales*, 24 (Winter 1946), 10–14 (p. 10); *Quite Early One Morning* (London: J.M. Dent, 1954), 21–28 (p. 21). Garlick also uses the phrase as epigraph to 'Poem', *The Welsh-Speaking Sea*, 37.

71 Compare R.S. Thomas's statement here with his comment in a review in 1967 of William T. Moynihan's *The Craft and Art of Dylan Thomas* (1966): 'Many people would admit that Thomas wrote some eight or nine fine lyrics, and that on their testimony alone he can be rated a major lyric poet. But if they dismiss the rest of the poetry, this is resented by Thomas' devotees as somehow a detraction from his reputation'; *Critical Quarterly*, 9, 4 (Winter 1967), 382.

72 Ezra Pound, *Pisan Cantos* LXXXI, *The Cantos* (London: Faber and Faber, 1975), 520–21.

73 See Tony Brown, 'R.S. Thomas's Elegy for Dylan Thomas', *The Review of English Studies*, New Series, 51, 203 (2000), 451–55.

74 Walford Davies and Ralph Maud (eds.), *Dylan Thomas: The Collected Poems 1934–1953* (London: J.M. Dent, 1996), 88. R.S. Thomas's allusion to 'Poem in October' was first noted by Tony Conran in *Frontiers in Anglo-Welsh Poetry*, 178, 188.

75 Further on the two Thomases, see Walford Davies, 'Bright Fields, Loud Hills and the Glimpsed Good Place: R.S. Thomas and Dylan Thomas', in M. Wynn Thomas (ed.), *The Page's Drift: R.S. Thomas at Eighty* (Bridgend: Seren, 1993), 171–210; Geraint Davies, 'A Tale of Two Thomases – Reflections on Two Anglo-Welsh Poets', in Horst W. Drescher and Hermann Völkel (eds.), *Nationalism in Literature/Literarischer Nationalismus: Literature, Language and National Identity* (Frankfurt am Main: Peter Lang, 1989), 289–97; Alistair Heys, 'Ambivalence and Antithesis: R.S. Thomas's Relationship with Dylan Thomas', *Welsh Writing in English: A Yearbook of Critical Essays*, 10 (2005), 52–72.

76 John Betjeman, Introduction to *Song at the Year's Turning* (London: Hart-Davis, 1955), 14.

77 Ibid.

78 See Davies (ed. and trans.), *Autobiographies*, 65.

79 R.S. Thomas, 'The Making of a Poem' (1969), in Anstey (ed.), *R.S. Thomas: Selected Prose*, 86. Cf. Thomas's comments in Gwyneth Lewis and Peter Robinson, 'An Interview with R.S. Thomas', *The Black and White Supplement* (March 1981), 19: 'When I write, I'm listening with an inner ear to the way it sounds. I build the poem up like that. And if there's a word too many, it goes into the next line. But the thing is that I never really wrote them to be read out loud'.

80 Betjeman, Introduction to *Song at the Year's Turning*, 14.

81 See Raymond Garlick, *Landscapes and Figures: Selected Poems 1949–63* (London: Merrythought Press, 1964), 19; Garlick, *Collected Poems*, 71.

82 Thomas, *Experimenting with an Amen*, 15; Thomas, *Collected Poems*, 487.

Further on Thomas's translation of Caledfryn's poem, see Davies, *Gororau'r Iaith*, 91–92.

83 Thomas, *Mass for Hard Times*, 22.

84 Ibid.

85 Thomas, *Pietà*, 32–34; Thomas, *Collected Poems*, 172–73.

86 John Carey, 'Prytherch', *New Statesman*, 17 June 1966, 894. Carey also expressed the opinion that 'For [Thomas's] best poems you have to go back to lyrics like "Cyclamen" and "Night and Morning" (both in the 1946 collection [*The Stones of the Field*]), which manage to come mint-clean out of the dog-eared corners of the language: "The wind was gentle and the sea a flower." If that looks easy, try it. After a few years you will settle for a less demanding occupation. Mr Thomas has, and not only in his poetry'; ibid.

87 Ted Hughes, *The Hawk in the Rain* (London: Faber and Faber, 1957), 18.

88 On the affinities between Hughes's *Crow* and Thomas's work, see, for example, the following: 'R.S. Thomas Talks to J.B. Lethbridge', *The Anglo-Welsh Review*, 74 (1983), 54; Jeremy Hooker, review of *H'm*, *Poetry Wales*, 7, 4 (1972), 90; Colin Meir, 'The Poetry of R.S. Thomas', in Peter Jones and Michael Schmidt (eds.), *British Poetry Since 1970: A Critical Survey* (Manchester: Carcanet, 1980), 8–10 (see also the editors' comments in their Introduction, xxviii); Brown, *R.S. Thomas*, 74–75.

89 Thomas, *Residues*, 49.

90 Virginia Woolf, 'Dorothy Osborne's "Letters"', *The Common Reader*, Second Series (London: Hogarth Press, 1932), 59.

91 R.S. Thomas, *Not That He Brought Flowers* (London: Hart-Davis, 1968), 18.

92 See R.S. Thomas, *Abercuawg* (Llandysul: Eisteddfod Genedlaethol Cymru, 1976), and Anstey (ed.), *R.S. Thomas: Selected Prose*, 122–33. See also the poem 'Abercuawg' in R.S. Thomas, *Frequencies* (London: Macmillan, 1978), 26–27; Thomas, *Collected Poems*, 340–41.

93 *Dock Leaves*, 4, 11 (Summer 1953), 9. The poem was subsequently published in Thomas, *Poetry for Supper*, 9–13; Thomas, *Collected Poems*, 69–72. See Davies, *Gororau'r Iaith*, 62–63 for a discussion of this section of 'Border Blues' and of Thomas's letter of 31 December 1953.

94 Raymond Garlick, Editorial, *Dock Leaves*, 8, 22, p. 4.

95 Garlick, *A Sense of Europe*, 103; Garlick, *Collected Poems*, 47. 'Hermit of the Rocks', 'Apologia' and 'The Greeting' are, significantly, grouped together in *Collected Poems* (pp. 46–47).

96 Garlick, *Travel Notes*, 19.

97 See also David Lloyd, 'An Interview with Raymond Garlick', *Poetry Wales*, 26, 3 (January 1991), 37–38. The interview was republished in David T. Lloyd, *Writing on the Edge: Interviews with Writers and Editors of Wales* (Amsterdam & Atlanta, GA: Rodopi, 1997), 23–31.

98 Raymond Garlick, 'A Small Boy in the Thirties – 2', *Planet*, 103 (February/March 1994), 42–43.

99 Raymond Garlick, 'A Disagreement Between Friends', *Planet*, 147 (June/July 2001), 55–58.

100 Davies (ed. and trans.), *Autobiographies*, 23.

101 Garlick, 'Notes for an Autobiography', *Collected Poems*, 153.

102 Thomas, *Poetry for Supper*, 13; Thomas, *Collected Poems*, 72.

103 See, for example, Garlick's use of the quotation from 'Border Blues' in the following: *An Introduction to Anglo-Welsh Literature* (Cardiff: University of Wales Press, 1970), 6; 'A Disagreement Between Friends', 56; Editorial, *Dock Leaves*, 6, 18 (Winter 1955), 3. See also Raymond Garlick and Roland Mathias (eds.), *Anglo-Welsh Poetry 1480–1980* (Bridgend: Poetry Wales Press, 1984), 37.

104 Davies (ed. and trans.), *Autobiographies*, 22.

105 Idris Davies, 'Rhywle yng Nghymru', in Dafydd Johnston (ed.), *The Complete Poems of Idris Davies* (Cardiff: University of Wales Press, 1994), 97. See also Dafydd Johnston, 'Idris Davies a'r Gymraeg', in M. Wynn Thomas (ed.), *DiFfinio Dwy Lenyddiaeth Cymru* (Caerdydd: Gwasg Prifysgol Cymru, 1995), 101.

106 *Dock Leaves*, 6, 17 (Summer 1955), 17.

107 Garlick, *The Welsh-Speaking Sea*, 46; Garlick, *Collected Poems*, 20. Referring to the experience of putting together his *Collected Poems*, Garlick remarked: 'the mainspring of the poetry . . . is the anguish and laceration of physical disability, the messing up of life from early childhood on, its effects on temperament, lifestyle, relationships, work, the daily recoil from and rejection of it by the self, and equally the daily need (since life itself is the only meaningful absolute value) to survive it. Paradoxically, these negatives have given rise to the positive – poetry, the celebration of life, and poetic form, an elegant structure to counterbalance the body's loss of symmetry'; 'Easing the Tension: John Barnie Interviews Raymond Garlick', *Planet*, 62 (April/May 1987), 56.

108 John Wain, 'Green Fingers: To Elizabeth Jennings in Oxford', *Letters to Five Artists* (London: Macmillan, 1969), 55.

109 It is interesting to note that Tony Conran has seen Raymond Garlick's response to the 'triple catastrophe' he endured at the end of the 1970s (the break-up of his marriage, his loss of faith and the failure of the campaign for political devolution for Wales) in terms of his 'experiencing again the wound of his lameness, only this time as a crisis in his world-view, not simply in his physical being'; Tony Conran, '*Poetry Wales* and the Second Flowering', in M. Wynn Thomas (ed.), *A Guide to Welsh Literature, Volume VII: Welsh Writing in English* (Cardiff: University of Wales Press, 2003), 240.

110 Garlick, Editorial, *Dock Leaves*, 8, 22, p. 5.

Commission

for Raymond Garlick

Welsh not by birth, but for a better reason –
Birth being compulsory and not chosen,
As you chose this: to live here and be kind
To our speech, learning it, and to our race,
Who have God's pardon but have not His peace –
You know our grievance, know the bitter poison,
Black as despair, seeping from the wound
Your country dealt us; plead our rightful case
To those who come to us for what we give,
Who take and leave us ruined by their taking,
Since we must give in ways they understand.
They cannot see, the stale prerogative
Of history foists them on our luckless land;
Open their eyes, show them the heart that's breaking.

R.S. THOMAS

(Published in *Dock Leaves*, 6, 17 (Summer 1955), p. 17)

The Letters
1951–1999

1

Manafon • Montgomery
29.vi.51

Dear Mr Garlick,

I was interested in your discussion on the radio some weeks ago and glad that you managed to say one or two necessary things in the short time at your disposal. I am very concerned over the lack of journals etc. in Wales which provide a forum for English writing about Wales – as it frustrates some promising writing and also deprives the Welsh movement of what could be a very powerful ally. I hope you can keep your magazine going and keep it on the right track. I am enclosing 6/6 for the next 3 numbers, if you will kindly hand it to your treasurer.

Please let me know if I can help in any way – reviewing or any contributions. I will try to get the county library in Newtown to take a copy, if they do not already do so.

Yours sincerely,

R.S. Thomas

2

Manafon • Montgomery
10.vii.51

Dear Mr Garlick,

Many thanks for your kind letter. I hope you can continue with 'Dock Leaves' – I would suggest that you keep it small, but rich.

I don't know if the enclosed poem would suit: I hope to bring out a limited edition of poems in the autumn.

Yours sincerely,

R.S. Thomas

3

[Postcard]

Manafon
2.x.51

Many thanks for the copies of 'Dock Leaves'.
I hope you can maintain your admirable punctuality.

R.S. Thomas

4

Manafon • Montgomery
29.12.51

Dear Mr Garlick,

I enclose a copy of my last book for the kindness of a review.

Sincerely,

R.S. Thomas

5

The County Infirmary • Newtown • Mont.
24.1.52

Dear Mr Garlick,

Thank you for your kind letter. I have been exploring a new landscape lately. I had an operation for hernia a fortnight today – but am due up for a while tomorrow. Bed is very tedious, especially as one never gets through anything like the amount of reading that one would like.

Yes, Miss Crocker can complain that she tried to teach me English – I left there in 1932. It was Holyhead itself that made me what little of a poet I am. A horrible little town, with a glorious expanse of cliff and coastal scenery. I shall never outgrow my hiraeth for it.

I am looking forward to hearing your talk on Saturday. I would like to visit Spain if I had the money. Good luck in your new house.

Sincerely,

R.S. Thomas

6

Manafon • Montgomery
19.2.52

Dear Mr Garlick,

Thank you for your kind letter. I shall be off to London any day now to be cured of my extreme nationalism!

If you are having good discussions about 'gnawing the carcase' etc. I don't see why I should put a stop to them by explaining what I mean! After all, so much poetry is the result of a mood.

However, I should think most 'Anglo-Welshmen' who really know their country are ambivalent towards it.

I would like to boast that no one loves the old things of Wales more than I do, and yet there is something fearful sometimes in thinking 'ni bydd diwedd byth ar sŵn y delyn aur'.

Yours sincerely,

R.S. Thomas

7

Manafon • Montgomery
19.4.52

Dear Mr Garlick,

I will review the book if you like. I am not a very competent reviewer, however.

I should have ordered a copy of Mr Mathias' book – but I am so hard up that I have almost ceased buying books.

Yours sincerely,

R.S. Thomas

P.S. Thank you for reviewing mine.

8

Manafon • Montgomery
18.5.52

Annwyl Gyfeillion,

Roedd yn wir garedig ohonoch i'm croesawu yn eich cartref hapus ym Mhenfro. Diolch yn fawr.

Dychwelais yn ddiogel nos Wener, ond bu rhaid imi fynd i ffwrdd ddoe eto.

Gwelais yr hen gyfaill D.J. yn Abergwaun a chael sgwrs ddifyr a chroeso gan Mrs Williams – ac ymlaen â mi wedyn trwy Aberystwyth i Fanafon.

Yn bur,

R.S. Thomas

9

Manafon
27 May [1952]

Dear Mr Garlick,

I have done what I can with Mathias' poems. The book was delayed a day in the post.

I don't know whether the Tourist poem is of any use to you – you can print it if it is.

Yours sincerely,

R.S. Thomas

10

Manafon • Montgomery
4 July [1952]

Dear Mr Garlick,

Thanks for the card. 'Y Faner' asked me to review Mathias'
book. I explained that I had done so for you, but they didn't
think it mattered, so I gave them a sort of Welsh rendering of
what will appear in Dock Leaves.

I came across the word 'pash' in rereading Hopkins – so
Mathias has a high authority for his use of the word –
nevertheless it seems unfortunate to me.

Some visitors called so I got merely a fragment of your
radio ode. I hope you were pleased with it – the whole thing is
a bit questionable as people rarely listen to verse for so long –
but there you are – 30 gns are quite useful!

Sincerely,

R.S. Thomas

11

Manafon
21.ix.52

Dear Raymond Garlick,

Thank you for your kind letter. I was astonished at the B.B.C.'s rendering of my 'pryddest'. I thought they read it appallingly. Only the girl showed any intelligence in her approach to it. I can't think how you got anything out of it at all, and feel you are just being kind. The B.B.C. read verse shockingly, I think.

I am glad you got over to Dublin. Sorry you didn't manage to call here. We were in Holyhead early in August, but were put off by the hordes from crossing to Eire.

I don't think I shall be at Pencader. The situation calls for something more than singing nostalgic songs around a tomb stone. Think of what they could do with all the petrol money.

But, of course, every political party must have its outings. What horrifies one is that the Blaid ones are never larger than a village flower show.

I'm no politician myself, so shouldn't talk – but I wonder sometimes if they have really looked the situation in the face.

Best wishes to you both.

Sincerely,

R.S. Thomas

12

Dear Mr + Mrs Garlick,

I was hoping to send my booklet – The Minister – for Christmas, but I fear it will not be out in time. So I will send later. Meanwhile Nadolig bendigedig i chwi eich dau.

I heard your reviews last night. The time given was preposterous. 5 minutes for Dylan Thomas' Collected Poems!

I don't think Hopkins was really Welsh-speaking.

Yn gynnes,

R.S. Thomas

13

Manafon • Montgomery
12.1.53

Dear Raymond Garlick,
    Thank you for sending your poem. I am glad to have it. I have delayed acknowledging it in the hope that my own thing would be ready – but have to write before you think bad things of me.
    I will send my renewal subscription next time I write.

Yours sincerely,

R.S. Thomas

I was delighted to hear about the little boy – he is very lucky.
I made a sermon on it – The adoption.

14

Manafon • Montgomery
13.4.53

Dear Raymond Garlick,

Thanks for the Dock Leaf. I forgot to pay, so do so now. I hope the enclosed pot-pourri is not too long for the next issue. I am glad to hear of Iestyn's progress.

Yours sincerely,

R.S. Thomas

15

Manafon
Aug. 13 [1953]

Dear Raymond Garlick,

Thank you for the copies of Dock Leaves and for noticing 'The Minister'.

We were at the sea for a fortnight with Gwydion and now I am cumbered with much gardening which leaves no time. The Roman Catholics have made a pleasant church at Gellilydan near Maentwrog. They converted an old building.

Yours sincerely,

R.S. Thomas

16

Manafon
7.xii.53

Dear Raymond Garlick,

Thank you for your letter. I am glad to hear good news of Iestyn. Gwydion is in his first term at preparatory school.

I don't feel I have anything original I can say about Dylan Thomas. I don't fancy myself as a critic I am afraid. He wrote a few major lyrics but I don't feel his work has sufficient facets to lend itself to detailed analysis.

However if anything comes before February, I will send it.

I have to give a talk in Cardiff on February 9th and if the weather is open, my wife and I might take a day or two and come home via Pembrokeshire. But this is in the air. After such a wild beginning I expect blizzards and arctic temperatures after Christmas – that does not affect the mild Welsh sea board – but it can make the interior difficult if not impassable.

Yours sincerely,

R.S. Thomas

I liked your poem in Time + Tide some months ago.

17

Manafon • Montgomery
15.xii.53

Dear Raymond Garlick,
   It is very kind of you to offer a night's hospitality to my wife and myself. I am sure Mrs Garlick has more than enough to do with Iestyn, without taking in vagabonds from the north. However, I will let you know nearer the time what our itinerary is likely to be. If wintry, it is likely to be I solo to Cardiff and back by train!
   Thank you very much for your leaflet of poems. I wish I could have shown so much achievement at your age.
   It is good to see you striving for an individual means of expression. Wales should be grateful that an Englishman has dug his feet so firmly into the country of his adoption.
   As you go on you will, I am sure, eliminate the echoes of other people's voices, discipline your easy rhymes, and refine your alliterative and assonantal obviousness. I say that at the risk of making you angry – because you did not ask for criticism.

   With all good wishes for Christmas joy from

R.S. Thomas

18

Manafon
31.xii.53

Dear Mr + Mrs Garlick,

Thank you very much for your Christmas greetings. It was a change to receive some real verse on a Christmas card. I hope you had an enjoyable time in London.

Gwydion is home now. We have just endured a pantomime for him. We go all the way to Shrewsbury to imbibe three hours of English proletarian culture.

However as there is no Welsh culture to put in its place – there it is.

That is why we sent him to an English boarding school. We haven't even a national dress for him. This is the more bitter, as two of the boys at his school are Scotch and wear the kilt on Sunday.

Every blessing on the three of you in 1954.

R.S. Thomas

19

Manafon • Montgomery
3.2.54

Dear Mr + Mrs Garlick,

As I feared the weather is bad. I am due in Cardiff next Tuesday to speak. If the weather gives I will go by road and my wife will come with me. We should then come on to Pembrokeshire and would be very glad to stay with you Thursday night, if we could put you to such inconvenience. If, however, the weather remains wintry I will have to go down to Cardiff and back by train alone, and we will see you some other time.

I will let you know more definitely over the weekend, as one may know by then if it is giving or not.

The roads are atrocious. We are without telephones – and this is all the paper I have!

Pob bendith,

R.S. Thomas

I thought – Under Milk Wood – excellent.

20

Manafon • Montgomery
7.2.54

The thaw has now arrived, so my wife and I rather think to come by car. It would be nice to stay with you Thursday night. If this is inconvenient, write me at Moelwyn Merchant's, Llanhenog, CAERLLEON, Monmouth.

Yn bur,

R.S. Thomas

21

Manafon • Montgomery
13.2.54

Dear Mr + Mrs Garlick,

Thank you so much for your kindness in allowing us to break our journey at Tŷ Mair. We had a sousing as far as Abergwaun, then the rain lifted and the mountains showed us what further north can do. We were glad to find Iestyn coming along so well.

Bendithion lawer,

R.S.T.

22

Manafon
14.iv.54

Dear Raymond Garlick,

Thank you for your letter. I am glad you have managed to get to a Welsh district if that is what you wanted. Blaenau is an unhealthy place, I believe, so I should <u>strongly</u> advise you to seek a house outside – say Manod or better still Llan Ffestiniog, or best of all Maentwrog, though that is getting a bit far from school. Nevertheless, the buses are fairly good in that district, I believe.

I hope you will be happy. My own feeling is the north for scenery, the south for people. We are an uncourageous race. I always feel a certain sympathy with Gildas. A man once said to my father when he arrived in Holyhead: Be friendly with all, intimate with none. Sound advice! The man was not Welsh! You will not find it easy to keep your dignity among a Welsh community.

Emyr Humphreys is at Pwllheli Grammar School – if you could meet with him some time it might be to your mutual advantage.

If we can do anything to help at Whitsun in the way of beds, let us know. I am afraid we are not on your route unfortunately – but you are very welcome.

Sincerely,

R.S. Thomas

23

Manafon • Montgomery
17.vi.54

Dear Raymond Garlick,

I don't know whether you have got your stuff for the next Dock Leaves, or whether you would care to have the enclosed.

Have you been up to Blaenau Ffestiniog yet or not? And if so, were you successful in finding quarters? I hope Iestyn and Mrs Garlick are well. Saturday is half term for Gwydion so we shall be seeing him this weekend.

Sincerely,

R.S. Thomas

24

Manafon • Montgomery
23.viii.54

Dear Raymond Garlick,

Thank you for your letter and the poem pamphlet.

We have been spending a week on Ynys Enlli and returned only on Saturday night.

I don't like the poems but can see your point about the promise. There is a certain control of the movement. He does not seem to have anything to say at the moment, but is merely playing with words. However that is not a vice in a young poet.

I am glad you are settled in your new home and trust it is out of the town since you mention sheep. Trawsfynydd + Maentwrog are fine. We stayed a night at the latter on our way to Enlli.

We are leaving Manafon in October, for Eglwys Fach, Sir Aberteifi, between Machynlleth + Aberystwyth.

Cofion fil,

R.S. Thomas

25

[Postcard]

Manafon
9.x.54

Thank you for your letter. Yes, include the tractor if you wish.
We are moving to Eglwys Fach, Machynlleth, on Monday.
Glad you are settled at Blaenau.

Cofion,

R.S. Thomas

26

Eglwys Fach • Machynlleth • North Wales
13.xii.54

Dear Raymond Garlick,

Thank you very much for the copy of P.B.M. I am sorry you had not included one of your own – but I suppose that is one of the penalties of being an editor.

We are settling down here gradually and hope you are doing the same. I trust the school is not too grim. Blaenau in this weather must be pretty gloomy.

It is an ugly house we have here. I hope you were more fortunate. The district is superb, however. The Welsh tends to be weak, but at least one speaks it everyday, unlike Manafon where I never used it.

Rupert Hart-Davis are bringing out Selected Poems for me next year – so I hope the necessity for publishing my own stuff is over. If I don't write before Christmas – pob bendith arnoch eich tri yn ystod gŵyl eni'r Iesu.

R.S.T.

27

Eglwys Fach • Machynlleth • North Wales
31.xii.54

Dear Raymond Garlick,
　　Thank you for your copy of P.B.M. and your own poems. I am glad you have been able to get some of your work into a book. It is about the only way these days – at least to start with. Stockwell and Fortune are to be avoided. I hope you don't think I am patronising or condescending. I happen to be several years older than you and have had to work and try and fail, and am still far from any sort of goal. So when I say your work has promise, you can understand, if you like, that it has far more promise than mine showed at your age. The last poem, Biographical Note, seems to me to show that most clearly. You must get over your exaggerated regard for Dylan Thomas – he is a bad influence – a better sign post than map. He wrote some half dozen first class lyrics – the rest is dross.

Best wishes to you all in 1955.

R.S. Thomas

28

Eglwys Fach • Machynlleth • North Wales
27.vi.55

Dear Raymond Garlick,

I wonder whether you have gone to press for your next number, or whether you would like to have this.

I was so glad to find you happily settled in your new home and to hear the Welsh ripening on Iestyn's lips.

Sincerely,

R.S.T.

29

Eglwys Fach • Machynlleth • North Wales
18.x.55

Dear Raymond Garlick,

Thank you for your kind letter. The interior of the book – the set up, I mean, is all right. I do not take much to the cover and the printing of the title I positively dislike – but there we are.

I felt uneasy about my own contribution to the last D.L. I am always promising to write a Welsh Hanrahan's Song about Wales – but it never really comes off. One gets pleased at the time and then turns a sour look on the thing later. The muse will not be forced.

Cofion,

R.S.T.

30

Eglwys Fach • Machynlleth • North Wales
22.xii.55

Dear Raymond + Elin Garlick,

I hope you will be happy this Christmas and that Iestyn will be well and jubilant in the Lord who made little creatures like him as well as hardened sinners like oneself.

I failed to hear you the other night on the air, as I had to go out. I hope it went off all right and that you were satisfied.

Gwydion is home with us now and seems well and cheerful, having distinguished himself by being bottom of his form! However, as he was only moved into it last term, we must not grumble.

They tell me 'The Minister' is going to be done on the 3rd Program at some future date. I am hoping they do it better than the Welsh Reg.

Cofion cu a phob bendith,

R.S.T.

31

Eglwys Fach • Machynlleth • North Wales
17.1.56

Dear Raymond Garlick,

Thank you very much for the copy of Dock Leaves – not at all 'dark' as Hart-Davis would have it!

It is very good of you to devote so much space to my book and I feel most unworthy of it.

It was bad luck about the influenza. I hope all is well now.

Gwydion goes back to school to-day. We are having trouble with our old car, and are faced with the expense of trying to get a new one. Gwae ni! When that is over perhaps I shall see you again.

All good wishes,

R.S.T.

I hold your calligraphy up to Gwydion as an example!

32

Eglwys Fach • Machynlleth • North Wales
22.2.56

Dear Raymond Garlick,

One of the things I have been meaning to tell you is to drop the Mr. – Thomas, or Ronald, or R.S. – anything rather than that millstone of age round my neck.

I shall be pleased to take part in your discussion. I never refuse the BBC as I am always in need of the cash, although I have felt many times I ought to on the score of integrity!

I had better come and see you perhaps when this weather breaks so that we can sketch out what we want to say.

I hope Iestyn remains well. You must find the hills a trial this weather.

Yn bur iawn,

R.S.T.

33

Eglwys Fach • Machynlleth • North Wales
25.ii.56

Dear Raymond Garlick,

I can see it's going to be difficult to meet as I have one or two things on, and Elsie has the car Wednesdays and Thursdays.

I think the best plan is to forego an earlier meeting and arrange a recording at Bangor. We could then discuss the thing for a while before the recording. What sort of a meeting have you on March 17? If it is not an exhausting one, perhaps we could get the BBC to record that day. I could pick you up on the way and drop you on the way back. If you are in school all the week I cannot see any other day for it. But let me know how you are placed.

We have changed our old car for a small Austin Van, with seats for the driver and one passenger, so you see I can manage one but no more.

Yn bur,

R.S.T.

34

Dear Raymond Garlick,

I can't manage next Saturday. Let us hope the BBC and you can fit in the 17th. If not I shall have to come to the live broadcast on the 21st. But I can't have the car that night, and it means changing my Lent service, all for 10 minutes on the BBC!

Betjeman's remarks to which you refer are almost drivel and are not a true statement of my views at all. To say Yeats influenced me and in the same breath to say I don't believe in reading aloud is rubbish. Neither do I shun the XIX Century as Betjeman says I do. The remark about the inner ear is a poetic platitude.

I shall expect to hear from you as to what arrangement you come to with Bangor.

Yn bur,

R.S.T.

35

Eglwys Fach • Machynlleth • North Wales
9.iii.56

Dear Raymond Garlick,

 I think record at 7.30 on March 21st if you can manage. I can probably get the car after all, so could pick you up on the way and leave you to make your own way back if that would help. If you would prefer, however, I don't mind doing a live broadcast, so it's up to you. Re. the other points I will do as you say, but will try to avoid quotations as far as possible.

Yours sincerely,

R.S.T.

I hope the play succeeds.

36

Eglwys Fach • Machynlleth • North Wales
19.iii.56

Dear Raymond Garlick,
 I shall hope to arrive about 4.0 p.m. on Wednesday – so shall look forward to seeing you somewhere about then at Bryn Awel. My schedule from BBC says rehearsal at 6.0, so plenty of time.

Yn bur,

R.S.T.

*   *   *

Radio somewhat of a return to pre-printing press days, or at least to days when poets read their work aloud and were not read by others. Strictly speaking, therefore, poets who have carried on the older tradition are the ones to have work broadcast. B.B.C. does not like short poems. Short poems should be read twice at least. So should difficult ones. 2 readers might read the same poem to give different interpretations. Poetry now seen to be an indissoluble marriage of form and content. To my mind, probably owing to contemporary habits, this more likely to appear on the page than via the ear. The sound therefore will tend to predom. over the meaning on the radio. Thus poems that derive value rather more from sound than meaning will be the most successful – e.g. Ballads by Watkins, etc.
 Also difference between average radio set and being viva

voce. Words never as clear. Sense of strain. Loss of valuable syllables, connections etc. Added to all this, however, the amount of time necessary to such perfection of medium suggests a much more settled order of society than obtains at present.

There is also the question of contemporary sounds as against traditional.

One personal objection to composing for the ear is arbitrary length of the metric line. Dylan Thomas' poems look very tidy on the page, but that metrical pattern was completely shattered when he read them aloud.

A weak metric line can also be bluffed across when reading aloud.

With regard to the reading itself, I am against the actor's style of reading according to sense, at least with every poem – it may be necessary with some. I prefer to retain a little of the metre at least.

I can see that some people and some voices suit some poems and not others – but I tend to a Yeatsian booming or sonorous style, which even if rather passé these days, seems to have been the tendency of poets, judging by recordings of Tennyson – and so on ad nauseam.

37

Eglwys Fach • Machynlleth • North Wales
14.xi.56

Dear Raymond Garlick,

I have been meaning to write for some time, but only now have succeeded!

I rehashed 'Border Blues' for the 3rd Programme, and they will be doing it on November 26th as far as I know. I am recording a short introduction to it at Swansea next Friday. I hope you don't mind, as in its written form it appeared in Dock Leaves a few years ago. It shows I'm finished, having to fall back on old work!

I hope things are well with you. It is not easy to see this Russian business sub specie aeternitatis. Wales is a bit astray about it, I think, or perhaps I am becoming Anglicised here.

Cofion,

R.S.T.

38

Eglwys Fach • Machynlleth • North Wales
23.xi.56

Dear Raymond Garlick,

I enjoyed your little extravaganza on Bangor and thought it went off well. The refrain was a good idea. I'm afraid my stay there was little more than a tune hummed thoughtlessly.

I should go slow with Keidrych. He can be an awkward customer on occasion. He is a mixture of many elements.

[ ] wrote to me, enclosing a poem. I replied as politely as I could. Since when I have received several poems, which, not being an editor, I have not returned!

Yn bur,

R.S.T.

39

Dear Raymond Garlick,

Thank you very much for your card and good wishes. I hope you had a happy time. Iestyn now taking an interest in Siôn Corn no doubt.

We had snow at Christmas as probably you did – not acceptable – too constant a reminder of Europe.

All good wishes for 1957.

From

R.S.T.

40

Eglwys Fach • Machynlleth • North Wales
31.v.57

Dear Raymond Garlick,

Thanks for your letter. I hope you enjoyed Rome. I met somebody yesterday who hopes to retire there one day.

I am afraid I pitched my talk out. It was only one of those things which one does for the B.B.C. when one is hard up.

I am glad to hear Iestyn progresses.

There seem to be so many things to do here that poetry recedes further and further into its corner.

Yours sincerely,

R.S.T.

41

Eglwys Fach • Machynlleth • North Wales
20.xii.57

Dear Raymond Garlick,

Just to hope that you will all have a happy time at Christmas. I always feel slightly smug and exclusive at Christian festivals. 'After all, my dear fellow, it is only people like you and me who really know what it is all about!' Still the secular approach is pretty grim. We have strayed a long way from the poverty and simplicity of the manger.

I am sure Iestyn has developed a lot by now. I hope you are still happy in Blaenau. I have not been that way for some time. Would you be good enough to send on my belated Dock Leaves sub. next time you write south?

Pob bendith,

R.S.T.

42

Dear Raymond Garlick,

Thank you for sending along your poem 'Blaenau Observed'.

I am glad you have found a more congenial home and hope you will settle down there. I am sure it will be all to the good of Blaenau and its school, if you can. I suppose that for an artist in the modern world, life is a succession of upheavals. Certainly I spend most of my time coping with situations and trying to re-acclimatize myself to poetry in the brief intervals between.

Sometimes I think Rome is right – plain song, the splendour of the Mass, the incorporation of folk cult (as the dance in Spain) and then the thought of Rome as she is represented in places like Machynlleth suggests that there is nothing between us in some places and at some levels. Certainly one longs sometimes for some ritual to conceal the poverty (not simplicity) of the reformed services with their stress on language which few understand now, even if they did once. But it seems on the whole that in Britain one can only have these things where there is sufficient population. I am afraid the rural church has always been somewhat the same.

You addressed a letter from a Bangor student to me asking for a visit. I wish they would state a fee when they write. The universities have plenty of money. Aberystwyth offered 6 guineas when I spoke there. (This in case the man lives in Blaenau!)

With all good wishes for 1958 from

R.S.T.

I hope you have no more trouble with your foot.

43

Dear Raymond,

It was good of you to mention Poetry for Supper in your editorial – I don't suppose Hart-Davis sent you a copy. I don't know to whom he sends them. I hope the Anglo-Welsh Review is holding its own. I am sorry Wales started up again. There is not room for the two, I'm afraid. Keidrych asked me for something, but I did not accept. I saw James Hanley the other night. I had not been over for about a year, I'm afraid.

I hope things are going along fairly well with you and that you still like Blaenau.

Good wishes to you all over Easter.

From

Ronald

44

Eglwys Fach • Machynlleth • North Wales
8.x.58

Dear Raymond,

Thank you for your kind letter. You mustn't ever feel you are intruding. I shall be glad to see you any time you are passing. And certainly you must keep up the struggle with your own muse, despite the claims of Blaenau secondary school on your time.

I am sorry to hear about Mr McCoye and hope he can be mended poor thing.

Yours sincerely,

Ronald

45

Eglwys Fach • Machynlleth
[Christmas 1958]

Dear Raymond,

Just a line to wish you and your family happiness at Christmas. I don't send cards. I don't like hilarious Santas and over-red robins to try to speak for me. In fact it is a pleasure to greet a fellow Christian at Christmas and to know that he will be thinking in terms of something other than his belly.

And may peace, and peace and peace be everywhere.

Ronald

46

Eglwys Fach • Machynlleth • North Wales
[Christmas 1959]

Dear Raymond,

Just a line to wish you all happiness at Christmas. I hope everything goes pretty well with you. I feel uncomfortable about you and 'Wales'. There doesn't seem to be room for 2 journals. I wish Keidrych hadn't re-started. He had the cheek to say in an interview the other night that he thought his present contributors better than his original ones. He rang up and asked if he could reprint my Christmas article which appeared in Vogue 3 years ago. I notice it appeared without acknowledgment!

I hope the Muse visits you now and then. She seems to leave me mostly alone – but probably this is mainly my fault, as I took advantage of the lovely summer to be out + about birding + botanising a good deal.

With every good wish for Christmas + 1960 from

Ronald

47

Dear Raymond,

Yes, certainly give my name for what it is worth. Unfortunately I know no one in that department. I know only Gwyn Jones + Cecil Price in the English department.

I sincerely hope you are successful.

I'm sorry you did not call yesterday if you were passing.

Yours sincerely,

Ronald

48

Eglwys Fach • Machynlleth • North Wales
3.x.60

Dear Raymond,

I have been wondering whether you were successful in your application for a lectureship. Let me know when you have time what became of your efforts.

I expect you have been gallivanting the continent again this summer. We went down to Llŷn and Gwydion and I had a week on Bardsey.

I hope you are all well.

Yours sincerely,

Ronald

49

Eglwys Fach • Machynlleth • North Wales
25.x.60

Dear Raymond,

I am sorry you are leaving, but I expect you are doing the right thing. Wales loses most of her best people for the same reasons, I'm afraid. But you are young and that is the time to do things, otherwise you get into a rut such as I have got into, where action is impossible for too many Coleridgean reasons.

I hope you will all be happy and successful in the Low Countries and not find them too low!

Yours sincerely,

Ronald

50

Eglwys Fach • Machynlleth • North Wales
19.xii.60

Dear Raymond,

I don't know whether you have left Wales yet, but send this to Blaenau in case you are still there. It is just to wish you the happiness or whatever word is appropriate to the peculiar atmosphere of Christmas. I could wish you had been going to some other country than Holland, but I suppose I am prejudiced in some ways. However, very few countries do appeal to me, and such as do are generally foisted on my imagination as being warmer or sunnier than some of the spells of weather that Wales can produce!

Iestyn must be quite a stout lad by now.

With best wishes to you all from

Ronald

51

Eglwys Fach • Machynlleth • North Wales
15.xii.61

Dear Raymond,

It was good to hear from you and to gather that on the whole you are happy – what is happiness? But you know what I mean. It's an awful thing this blood and soil, so against reason. Many's the time I start up and say why should I stay in this one-eyed country? Yet, I'm still here.

Yes, Hutchinson wrote to me for poems, and remembering some words of yours about 'Cynddylan on a Tractor' going down well with children, I sent that, which they took. As they asked me for other names, I suggested you. I'm sorry if you didn't have anything handy.

I hope you succeed over there. You are young enough and able enough to adapt. Science – mainly the bomb – has changed the surface things so quickly that any form of nationalism – except the right kind – is hopelessly archaic.

But this again with the mind, I suppose. 'Le coeur a ses raisons' – Anyhow, every blessing and kind thought this Christmas to you all.

From

Ronald

52

Eglwys Fach • Machynlleth • North Wales
23.viii.62

Dear Raymond,

Thank you for your card. I am going to Llŷn to-morrow Friday to fetch my wife + son home. I will call on the way about 10/15–30 a.m., hoping that's not too early. We could then have half an hour's talk, before I proceed.

If, however, you have planned to go off to-morrow, never mind – it is not far out of my way.

Yours sincerely,

Ronald

53

Eglwys Fach • Machynlleth • North Wales
19.xii.62

Dear Raymond,

Just my wishes to you all for Christmas + 1963. It was nice to see you in the summer and I hope you still flourish. I don't grudge you your hard winters, but perhaps envy you some of the birds which you get and we don't. Things go along much the same here. I have written a lot of bad poetry since I saw you. I can imagine what the critics will say if I publish another book. You know Cummings' line: As critics will upon a poet feast. It has a nice maggoty tang about it.

I hope your own muse is treating you more kindly.

Yours sincerely,

Ronald

54

Dear Raymond,

I did not hear from you this Christmas, but trust all is well with you.

My son, Gwydion, has been accepted by Magdalen College, where he will read English (of which he has done little, having taken his A Levels in Classics. However, he is now reading for A Level English). He was accepted for next autumn, but as he will not be 18 until the end of August, we got them to accept him for autumn 1964 instead. [...]

Would there be any chance of his coming to you for say January–July terms 1964? Are there any vacancies? Is it very expensive, or do you know of any reliable but lively families who do this? His French is half-way there. I think he ought to perfect his French and have experience of level-headed living, but the idea of his being adrift in France raises my scalp these days. If you can spare a while, I would be grateful to hear from you.

Cofion cynnes,

Ronald

55

Eglwysfach Vicarage • Machynlleth • Montgomeryshire
[1963]

Dear Raymond,

Many thanks for your kind and helpful letter. I always feel I should frame your calligraphic efforts. I also received a prospectus from your headmaster – for which please thank him.

I can see that it is out of the question for Gwydion, and in any case his stay at his present school is uncertain. He has now changed and likes it so much that he may well grow to be an old man there!

However, I would appreciate from you the address of the Lausanne institute, where Mathias' boy was.

I was glad to see a poem of yours in the anthology 'Here Today'. An unpleasant title, with its implied sequel!

With good wishes,

Ronald

56

Eglwys Fach • Machynlleth • Mont.
25.ix.63

Dear Raymond,

Thank you for your letter. I will certainly do anything I can. I was delighted to think of the possibility of your returning to Wales. We certainly need more of your kind. It won't be an easy decision because of the children and their incipient polyglottism, but I hope you will be guided aright.

Yours sincerely,

Ronald

57

Eglwys Fach • Machynlleth
30.xii.63

Many thanks for your card. Glad to see in A.-W. Review about your poem.

Any news of the Inspectorate?

Blwyddyn newydd dda, a phob bendith,

Ronald

58

29.vi.64

Many thanks for your long + interesting letter. I am down in Llŷn for a few days tidying up at the cottage.

Ronald

59

Eglwys Fach
21.viii.64

Dear Raymond,

Thank you very much for the dummy of your poems. I am honoured that you should send me one. I think I like 'Penumbra' best. I am sorry that I was apparently away when you and Elin called. Elsie and Gwydion were returning from a long stay in France, and I was down in Gower.

Yes, Lampeter wrote to me and were answered to the best of my poor ability. I also wrote a covering note to the Principal. But, of course, I have no influence. I hope you get it, however.

Yours sincerely,

Ronald

60

Eglwys Fach • Machynlleth
Christmas '64

Dear Raymond,

I infer from a general silence that you were not appointed to Llanbedr Pont Steffan. Their loss, I imagine. I'm sorry. It would have been nice to meet you occasionally, shopping in Aberystwyth, that Athens of Wales. However, I know you are happy in a way at Ommen and that is good. The children are probably being better educated than they would be round Llanbedr. A certain Mr. Stephens from Merthyr Tydfil is going to start Poetry Wales. He must be mad.

Gwydion has just returned from his first term at Magdalen, where he is supposed to be reading English. He doesn't think much of the lectures, but seems to like his tutor, which is a blessing.

Nadolig llawen i chwi i gyd,

Ronald

61

Eglwysfach Vicarage • Machynlleth • Montgomeryshire
27.xii.65

Dear Raymond,

It was good to get your long letter. Thank you very much. I was glad to know you were getting encouraging letters from publishers. I believe the position is still difficult, and then the books are safely buried with about 8 others in half a column in some paper or magazine, in order to make way for a half page review of some latest novel – 'a major work', 'brilliant' etc. etc.

I should stay in Holland, if you can stand the climate. I think there are certain hopeful things happening, but it is more and more becoming an annex of England, and a dormitory of the towns, while the summers are becoming more and more hectic and insanitary to the great glee of the Welsh tourist board. I'm afraid I got muddled as to whether I write to you at Christmas or for the New Year, so forgive me. I was in Denmark and Sweden in September and encountered Netherlanders birdwatching.

With all good wishes from

Ronald

62

Eglwysfach Vicarage • Machynlleth • Montgomeryshire
21.iii.66

Dear Raymond,

Many thanks for your letter. There is a long story behind that article, which I will not bore you with. Briefly it got into the hands of a 'colleague' in the editor's absence, who proceeded to 'edit' it! As it was already in the hands of the printers I let the thing pass, but several of my points and ways of phrasing were omitted.

The Anglican Church is also at it revising its services now, but as it takes them many years to alter a preposition, perhaps there is not so much to fear. I had heard from other Roman friends that they had been hard hit.

I'm sorry you drew a blank with Hogarth. It is so difficult to get them to risk much. Have you tried Hart-Davis? Rupert is always sympathetic, though I don't know how much he does now that he is living in Yorkshire. He goes to London now + again.

Yours,

Ronald

63

Eglwysfach Vicarage • Machynlleth • Montgomeryshire
3.x.66

Dear Raymond,

I was delighted to hear that you will be returning to Wales. I am sure it is your rightful place, despite the kicks and disappointments it entails. 'Duw a'm helpo, ni fedraf ddianc rhag hon.' Parry-Williams sums it up for all of us, really. Anyway it will be good to have you back, enriched with the experience you have gained.

I was grateful for your comments. As I think I said, the older I get, the less sure I feel. Loss of nerve? 'The writer's middle years' as Durrell calls them? A lyric poet soon loses his shine I fear and there is the awful struggle to 'concoct the old heroic bang' as Hughes puts it. You know as a poet how some poems go cold on one – a distressing feeling – and I'm afraid more poems in Pietà have done this than in any other book. The only one I'm sorry you don't like is Gospel Truth. The cohering theme is the way God i.e. love works out his purpose even in such weird folk as some of my Montgomery farmers. But evidently I have got lost among the characters, so that the wood is not visible for the trees. Anyway, it is good of you to write at such length – so much more helpful than the slick and spiteful half truths of the columnists.

I have said some sharp things about the English and the urban outlook, so must expect to be attacked. The trouble is in thinking one is important enough to be attacked. It is more likely that the work is after all just bad.

With all good wishes for the future,

Ronald

64

Eglwysfach Vicarage • Machynlleth • Montgomeryshire
18.xii.66

Dear Raymond,

Just a few lines of greeting to you all at Christmas – your last in Holland, I hope. It is good to think of you returning to Wales, and to a constituency that has a nationalist member, too. As the borders become more Anglicised, so the kernel of Wales becomes more definitely nationalist. I was over in Manafon a week ago marrying someone and found that odd people who used to speak Welsh now change into English after a sentence or two.

Never mind, it is an interesting time to be alive, if a trying and sad one.

I am sure you will be more satisfied in one way at Caerfyrddin, if dissatisfied in a thousand others!

Gyda phob dymuniad da i chi yn y flwyddyn newydd,

Ronald

65

Dear Raymond,

It was good of you to write. I got your letter at Trinity College, where I thought of you in residence in a few months' time. Euros told me that Childs listens to people like Ffowc Elis and Norah Isaac, so that could be good. It was good to go for a walk before breakfast past the awful housing estate, and watch two foxes following their noses in a large field facing me. I hope you will be happy and successful there. I am sure the students will appreciate you.

I am afraid Aberdaron is very vulnerable now, and the saints' road to Bardsey is a thoroughfare for ice cream vendors and consumers. However, it is a lovely area, and both Church-wardens actually write to me in Welsh.

Yours sincerely,

Ronald

66

Aberdaron • Pwllheli
[Summer 1967]

Dear Raymond,

It was nice to hear from you. I was just off on the last of my Eglwys Fach commitments when it came. I have cut down on all these, but unfortunately had promised to do one before I knew I was coming here. I have a pretty water-tight excuse now, although many have no real idea where Aberdaron is. What is nice is that the locals all seem to like being here so much. 'Dach chi'n leicio yma?' is the common question, and they all cackle with satisfaction when I reply 'Wrth fy modd'. Despite much English, that awful industrial twang, and quite a few settlers also, there is nevertheless plenty of Welsh, and it is good to be where it is still quite obviously the main medium of daily life.

I do hope you have got satisfactorily accommodated and that Iestyn will pass his A Level. We are awaiting the result of Gwydion's degree examination, which should be out the end of this week.

I agree that 'Welsh Voices' was not very good. I told, I think Bryn Griffith, some years ago that I didn't think there were many good young Anglo-Welsh writers, poets, that is, but he said he would prove the contrary.

Yours sincerely,

Ronald

67

Aberdaron • Pwllheli
[Christmas 1967]

Dear Raymond,

Thank you for your letter and kind wishes. I am so glad you have been able to adjust to a small room again. Its window opens on eternity. (Nice touch, that.) An eternity of what is the question.

It's hard to say down here at the end. I think there may be more Welsh consciousness in Eifionydd, but I'm disappointed in the atmosphere in Llŷn. It is the most servile to the English area I have come across. The effect of tourism and low employment. 'What would we do without the English?' They either can't or won't see that years of English government has failed to give them employment in their own area. A perfect argument for home rule – but no. My respect for Welsh intelligence grows less every year. The English outmanoeuvre them every time. This investiture will be worth much more than ½ million to England – otherwise they wouldn't touch it.

However, this area is superb and there are always the five for whose sake the city will not be destroyed.

Nadolig dedwydd i chi i gyd,

Ronald

68

Aberdaron • Pwllheli • Arfon
14.v.68

Dear Raymond,

Thank you for your letter. I have made inquiries and find that the Academi has been divided into two sections, but that members of either section are deemed to belong to Yr Academi Gymreig. So if I join the Welsh section as originally invited to do, the English section can still say that I am a member of the Academi. I hope this will meet the difficulty.

I'm afraid I can't think like you about bilingualism, although I realise that rationally speaking one tends to get outargued. It depends rather in what part of Wales one lives, I suppose. I can see that the bois bach in the south are in a bit of a jam, as, of course, I am, too, in having to write in English.

I'm glad of Iestyn's progress.

Yours sincerely,

Ronald

69

Dear Raymond,

Many thanks for your letter. I'm glad Gwasg Gomer are to publish your poems and that Iestyn progresses. I read Elin's articles in 'Barn' for the advancement of my learning.

I'm afraid I have no recollection of the interview or whatever it was to which you refer. I hope you are still happy at Caerfyrddin. I'm sorry you have lost Ffowc Elis, but hope there are other stalwarts there to make common cause with.

Yes, a new book of my poems called 'Not That He Brought Flowers' is due out this autumn. I decided that since a small number of people read me, there is no point in paying much attention to what the columnists say.

Yours sincerely,

Ronald

70

Aberdaron • Pwllheli
5.xi.68

Dear Raymond,

Very sorry to hear your bad news. Most worrying. The consolation is that he is young and nature may repair itself in conjunction with all the harmonious processes such as prayer, modern medicine, loving care and so on. I will contribute my quota. I always feel aggravated that I can't give more blood, since it is so needed. I have had a couple of shots, but have such a poor circulation that I have decided I am not the one to give any more. Perhaps I'm wrong. Anyway, I do sympathise and hope for better news. [. . .] I am sure you will go to London, if it becomes really necessary.

I will keep your Trinity students in mind, but I have been refusing all these invitations since coming out here.

Yours sincerely,

Ronald

71

Aberdaron • Pwllheli
16.xii.68

Dear Raymond,

I hope Iestyn is making progress. It's the most worrying Christmas you have had, I should think – just when things seemed to be settling down a bit for you. However, I don't suppose medical facilities were better in Holland than in London, where you can go presumably, should the need arise.

I hope things go well at Trinity College. I don't suppose you see much of Ffowc Elis now that he is immersed in the translation business. I hate translated poetry, although when one is unfamiliar with the original it can appear all right as in the case of Miroslav Holub.

It is good to be by the sea at Christmas, the real sea, although the idea of Christianity I am in touch with in this area is a long way from the XX Century, with the altar among the οἱ πολλοί.

With all good wishes for Christmas
to you and your household from

Ronald

72

Aberdaron • Pwllheli
15.iii.69

Dear Raymond,

I am horrified to see Feb. 4th on your last letter, but I don't think it came as long ago as that! I am sorry about Iestyn's slow progress. It must be very trying for you all, but I am glad he is having the best attention possible.

As you will see from the poem: And Prytherch, then, was he a real man? I have never been quite sure about his existence – he's certainly dead now! The first poem I wrote about him – A Peasant – certainly was written in the evening after visiting a 1000'-up farm in Manafon where I saw a labourer docking swedes in the cold, grey air of a November afternoon. I came later to refer to this particular farmer jestingly as Iago Prytherch.

Yours sincerely,

Ronald

73

Aberdaron • Pwllheli
25.iv.69

It was a kind thought to send the card of Bemerton, where 'prayer has been valid'. I hope all goes well and Iestyn's improvement continues.

R.S.T.

74

Aberdaron • Pwllheli
7.vii.69

Dear Raymond,

I am so glad to hear of Iestyn's improvement and long may it last. I was glad to get your letter, too. It is socially very lonely here. I don't suffer from loneliness, as I am always content to be alone in nature like the Celtic saints. But complete mental conformism in all one's neighbours can produce another kind of loneliness. They say there is quite a substantial vote for Y Blaid in this area, but I haven't come across it yet. As I have told you before, I am very disillusioned with Caernarfon as the 'most Welsh county in Wales'. Most of the County Council's business, correspondence, notices, Education Office, seem to be English, and people in the tourist areas such as Aberdaron are completely subservient to English interests and ready to turn savage with attitudes like mine, which to their one track minds mean a loss of revenue. In fact, as suspicions are getting about that I am a 'Welsh Nationalist', they are reacting with the uneasiness and incredulity of people with a traitor in their midst. I managed to get the Post Office to put up 'Y Llythyrdy' which my wife painted, but others, such as the butcher, just laugh uncomfortably at the suggestion that High Class Family Butcher looks a bit odd in Aberdaron. I suppose he thinks visitors confronted by a window full of sheep's carcases might not know what it was if it had Cigydd printed on top. I carry on endless correspondence with the County Council, because they will put up fresh monoglot signs – 'Whistling Sands' – without the original name 'Porth Oer'. No wonder signs get daubed. We can nail them now on the strength of Charlie Bach's attention to Welsh, but it doesn't change them. Nothing ever will.

Cofion,

Ronald

75

Aberdaron • Pwllheli
[Christmas 1969]

Dear Raymond,

Many thanks for your letter. I rejoice with you that Iestyn has made a good recovery. I wonder why it has to be Lourdes. Why not Ynys Enlli? In mediaeval times, as you know, three pilgrimages to Enlli equalled one to Rome. Now in the jet age, I should reverse the figures. I often see chastened bird-watchers mooching about the village waiting for the sea to abate so that they can cross. It's certainly a chancy place to get to.

I hope this letter reaches you. I have noted your move but lost (no, I've just found) your address. The ghost of Keidrych still lingers at Llanybri, I suspect.

Cofion cynnes at 1970,

Ronald

76

Aberdaron
11.v.70

Dear Raymond,

Thank you for the postcard and for your kind letter with its photographs. I can see what a strain it was, and only hope it is unrepeatable.

Yes, Edward Thomas wrote for something for his new venture. It shows how old I grow. I have seen many magazines start and peter out. You ask where should one go from Kierkegaard and I can only think back to Pascal, Augustine, Plato, except for Tillich, perhaps?

Yours sincerely,

Ronald

77

Aberdaron • Pwllheli
11.vii.70

Dear Raymond,

Thank you for your letter with its kind offer. It would be churlish to refuse, although I think you would be better employed in writing your own poetry. I see from the last Poetry Wales that you are learning to handle the stanza with more ease and assurance – if that doesn't sound too patronising!

The BBC asked me to speak about Bryncroes, and in true BBC style left out my 2 first points, beginning with number 3 and thus emasculating my argument. I then sent my main points to the Western Mail correspondence column, but presumably the letter was not printed. Viva, democracy.

Yours sincerely,

Ronald

78

Dear Raymond,

Good wishes to you and your family this Christmas – a strange world for the Incarnate God. I can't really locate him in the modern versions!

I hope Peter Thomas will persuade reasonable reactions among the die-hards on County Councils and such bodies, so that Iestyn and his friends may be spared the crudities of English prisons.

I hope you like Llansteffan and find its shores sufficiently staffed with herons.

This part of Wales is a dead loss to nationalism, and yet they speak Welsh as their first language and many of them vote Plaid apparently. But very conditioned in most ways – a strange mixture.

Yours sincerely,

Ronald

79

Dear Raymond,

I have signed your letter despite its bilingual heading! I don't suppose the English press will print it.

There seems something schizophrenic about Wales and its language being saved by the English language.

I had agreed against my better judgment to speak at the rally (rali in Welsh) in Aberystwyth. But, on receiving a letter from Dafydd Orwig Jones telling me he understood I was to address the meeting in English, I withdrew.

Despite all the difficulties and criticism and accusations of being unrealistic, I tend to side with Saunders on this question. After the initial boost to the Welsh ego, bilingualism means the end of Welsh as a creative language.

Cofion,

Ronald

80

Aberdaron • Pwllheli
10.viii.71

Dear Raymond,

Thank you for your last letter. I did not answer it sooner, as you said you were heading for the Eisteddfod. I'm sorry you are in trouble with the police. You should live in Llŷn, where they are all too busy being traffic wardens to have time for conspirators against the throne.

I was glad to hear that Iestyn is quite well again. That must be a relief.

My book will be published about March. I wish I could share your feeling that it is anything to look forward to!

Yours sincerely,

Ronald

81

Aberdaron • Pwllheli
[Christmas 1971]

Dear Raymond,

I hope you are en famille for Christmas. I grieve for people like Alwyn Gruffydd from the Pwllheli bookshop in that thugs' detention centre at Bryn Buga. The apathy of Aberdaron is cruel. All most of them think of is next spring with its fresh hordes of tourists. I got our Rural Deanery to sign a protest about the new marriage registration laws. Copies were sent to Peter Thomas, Goronwy Roberts, and the Registrar General. The first two have ignored us. Some minion at the General Register Office has requoted the rules to us, and told us how impracticable our suggestion is!

We must meet again and draft a fresh letter.

With all good wishes for Christmas + 1972,

Ronald

82

Dear Raymond,

I'm sorry to hear your bad news. It's enough to make one beat one's head on the wall, when there are all the crooks abroad, many of them in 'high office'. I happened to be in a house the other night, when the news was on the tele, and I noticed on the Northern Ireland bit how a van was ambling along with the back doors open ready for the troops to bundle some chance victim in so that the major could get a pat from the colonel and the colonel from the general + so on ad nauseam. The same thing in Wales – everyone afraid for his job, if a few arrests are not made.

I wrote to the New Statesman challenging him to devote a genuine article to the position in Wales, since the paper sets out to champion every other 'injustice' in the world. Needless to say, my letter was not published. We clergy of this deanery, who are protesting against the Registrar General's discrimination against Welsh, met Goronwy Roberts last Saturday and listened to him sermonising for 1½ hours. I don't suppose he'll achieve anything.

Kind thoughts,

Ronald

83

Aberdaron • Pwllheli
5.iv.72

Dear Raymond,

Thank you for your letter of before Easter with the report on Iestyn's illness. I hope all is now well on that account.

My wife, Elsie, developed shingles on her last visit to hospital, which has not helped. I wonder how matters progress with you. I listen to the wireless but seem to hear small news of any significance. Aberdaron is almost entirely without national consciousness. It seems to live by singing a few outmoded hymns in the winter, whilst waiting for the summer to bring in the English money.

Yours sincerely,

Ronald

84

Aberdaron • Pwllheli
26.viii.72

Dear Raymond,

Thank you for your letter. I am sorry not to have replied sooner but have been awaiting an answer from Macmillan's editor who has been on holiday.

My relationship with Hart-Davis has deteriorated considerably and they do not answer my letters now. Unfortunately certain terms in my contract are still binding. However, in May I sent them a formal request to reissue all my books. An American publisher has been negotiating with them for a collected or selected edition, but has got nowhere, it appears.

However, if they do not set about republication within nine months of my letter, the copyright will revert to me. I had consulted Macmillan in this connection.

Sorry about all this waffle. I hope you are all in good heart.

Yours sincerely,

Ronald

85

Aberdaron • Pwllheli
[Christmas 1972]

Dear Raymond,

I hope you are all together at Christmas and in one piece. I attended a meeting of Adfer in Penrhyndeudraeth and got the impression that Iestyn's stock was high. I hope you like your new principal, whoever he is, and that work, creatively that is, goes well. It is so much better here in winter, wild and undomesticated by the English with their dogs and children. Still it is an unenviable record that Wales has a greater proportion of television sets than the rest of Britain. So Aberdaron keeps in touch with the English, until they return in strength.

Gwyliau llawen,

Ronald

86

Aberdaron
Gŵyl Ddewi [1973]

Dear Raymond,

Better the day – Thank you for yours. I understand your unease. It is the number of fronts we are engaged on, and human inertia makes common cause with Civil Service obstinacy. I have been attacking the Governor of Albany gaol for refusing to pass on a letter of thanks to John Jenkins for sending me a Christmas card. I wrote to Peter Thomas and Goronwy Roberts and eventually got the usual glibly smug reply from the Home Office. Your letter prompted a riposte to the Home Office to reach them to-day.

I went to Fred Francis' welcome in Pwllheli. What a terrible speaker he is. A few adults had a meeting afterwards to see how we could help. I sent a memorandum to Aberystwyth – which was not acknowledged.

I don't mind going to Aberystwyth, but I can't be there Saturday night – Sunday, of course. Yes, Elsie is getting better thank you.

Cofion,

Ronald

P.S. After a lot of wrangling I have agreed to Hart-Davis publishing a selection from my 6 books by them. I was not prepared to see them re-published individually. This is 'promised' for the autumn.

R.S.T.

87

Aberdaron
20.iii.73

Dear Raymond,

Thank you for your kind note which came to-day. I was glad to see you had won a prize! Yes, I believe one ought to attend these functions, if one accepts the lucre. However, I have already booked a room in Cardiff, thank you.

I hope I manage to get there on Friday.

Yours sincerely,

Ronald

88

Aberdaron • Pwllheli
15.viii.73

Dear Raymond,

Thank you for yours. Yes, certainly add my name to your letter, but should it not be in Welsh? It is all so wearisome. My aged mother has just died – and the endless forms to be filled in, mostly in English, because that is the easiest and quickest way, and one gives in because time is short as one rushes from one office to another to catch some little gwas bach before he closes for the day after a couple of hours work! The registrar of deaths offered off his own bat to add the few words of Welsh underneath the English on the death certificate!

I hope to see you at Aberystwyth in September.

Cofion,

Ronald

89

Aberdaron • Pwllheli
31.viii.73

Dear Raymond,

I am a bit late in answering your kind letter of condolence – just the usual accumulation of chores which causes procrastination.

From what you once told me, you had even more difficulties in your relationship with your mother than I did. The strange workings of the female mind, if mind is the right word for it. However, mine became more tractable towards the end and there was mainly compassion.

Yours sincerely,

Ronald

90

Aberdaron • Pwllheli
[Christmas 1973]

Dear Raymond,

I hope things are moderately unagonising for you as a family this Christmas. I secretly rejoice that the Tories have got themselves into such a mess, but regret that a Labour government is the only alternative. Will the people of Wales never have enough of these two lying, incompetent giants? The things that Saunders was saying in Cwrs y Byd during the war are coming true, but later than he predicted. I suppose the money boys can still get together to make it all right for themselves.

I heard a rumour that Alwyn Rees had suffered a stroke. Such a necessary person in Wales; we can ill afford to have him hors de combat.

I wonder what sort of a Christmas this will be? I fear more crime and rushing about, if the factories are really going to be on short time. 'The wrong of unshapely things . . .'

With good wishes nevertheless,

Ronald

91

Dear Raymond,

I was glad to get your letter and to know that Alwyn is recovering – also to know that things are not too desperate with your family vis à vis the English law at the moment. John Jenkins sends me Christmas cards but I have no means of thanking him. The Governor of the prison returned my letters and although I wrote to the Home Secretary they dished out the usual pious twaddle. After this last Christmas I wrote to the chaplain of the gaol, whoever he might be, asking him to thank Jenkins from me. I had no reply. Perhaps he did, perhaps he didn't.

I turned the Claddagh people down. I had an Irishly unbusiness-like letter from John Montague about it.

Yours sincerely,

Ronald

92

Dear Raymond,

Greetings at Christmas. I hope all is well at Llansteffan as it is not at Sain Steffan. Here I float over the foundering British Empire wondering what fragments I can shore against my own ruin – un-Christmas-like thoughts brought on partly by the WNW gale which rages as I write. There are cool gales here all right, but no glades, nor enough trees to make a crowd. However we expect the Sunday School party here today, a handful of kids who will enjoy themselves in Welsh to my satisfaction in dulce jubilo.

Nadolig dedwydd i chi i gyd,

Ronald

93

Aberdaron
17.xii.75

Dear Raymond,

Christmases don't get any better externally, so one tries to warm oneself at an interior fire. I know you do too. Much health therefore, to you and yours.

If our enemies force a referendum, that will be farewell to home rule. Still, it is no time to take over the riddled economy which generations of English greed, arrogance and unwisdom have undone.

I am glad you are still writing. May the words continue to come. I hope you are all well.

Sincerely,

Ronald

94

Aberdaron • Pwllheli
7.1.76

Dear Raymond,

Thank you for your letter. I was very sorry to hear your news. Women have their own ways of justifying their actions, but, as Yeats says, eat a crazy salad with their meat. A birding friend of mine is a manic depressive of sorts. When he was discharged from hospital last year, his wife greeted him with the news that she was leaving him. In this case it was for another man, and there were no children. It is certainly wise and noble of you to keep the home going for the latter's sake. No amount of explaining on your part and understanding on theirs can substitute for the loss of a home, and, as you know, so many of the misfits and mesalliances are themselves from broken homes. I wish you all grace and blessings in your lonely task of doing that and continuing to write poetry.

Yours sincerely,

Ronald

95

Aberdaron
[Christmas 1976]

Dear Raymond,

Thank you for your letter. You sound rather dispirited, which is not surprising. These are dispiriting times. I was sorry to hear you were not writing poetry, however. I think it is a loss. As I said before, you were gaining mastery of the stanza and the ability to extend your matter.

I don't know what to make of the Welsh Department at Bangor. They were completely supine over the case of Y Cymric. Perhaps if Angharad presents them with a safe enough challenge, they may rise to it. It is materialism that is the undoing of the Welsh majority. They are too well off to want to risk a change. Aberdaron must be one of the most ignorant and obsequious parts of the country. And now we are to have the farce of a royal jubilee next year. An ignorant people will be exposed once again to the force and the guile of establishment propaganda. Strange thoughts at the Mass of Christ. 'My Kingdom is not of this world.'

Cofion,

Ronald

*

96

Aberdaron
31.viii.77

Dear Raymond,

Thank you for giving me your new address. I hope all goes well with you there and that Coleg y Drindod stays open.

Angharad is a lucky girl. I hope her car doesn't attract the wrong sort of man. I think I told you before that she and Iestyn inspired a Welsh sermon on the benefits of adoption.

I shall be 65 next March, so I shall perhaps not have so long in the Church, which seems to be taking the wrong turning. I was asked to go and bury Thomas Blackburn earlier this month. He had a cottage at Croesor. As I went up Cwm Croesor on a smiling August day, I was more than ever convinced that the world has taken a wrong turning, too.

I am trying to find out from Dafydd Wigley whether we can't arraign The Registrar General under the Race Relations Act for discriminating against the Welsh in the registration of marriages and deaths, but am not getting anywhere, I fear.

Ronald

97

Aberdaron
[Christmas 1977]

Dear Raymond,

Here are my poor Christmas wishes, a warm offering from a cold heart. A Christian has no right to be despondent, but there is a chill in the air out of the future.

I am retiring at Easter. I shall be 65. I could stay till 70, but I am glad to go from a Church I no longer believe in, sycophantic to the queen, iconoclastic with language, changing for the sake of change and regardless of beauty. The Christian structure is a meaningful structure, but in the hands of theologians or the common people it is a poor thing.

You will know that a group of us have formed a trust to buy Bardsey. We have signed the contract, but are going to have to raise £200,000 to pay for it and run it. So we are going to have a job to preserve its character of peace and seclusion.

I hope you have good news of Iestyn and Angharad.

Gyda chyfarchion,

Ronald

98

Dear Raymond,

This letter has several purposes:

1. to give you the address of a retired Christian.

2. to say that I am involved with the business of having bought Ynys Enlli. We have set up a trust to raise £200,000 and are trying in accordance with our articles of incorporation by the Charity Commissioners to keep parity between Natural History, Welsh and Christian interests. Do you think there would be any interest in the College for raising a bit of cash? I could send you some literature if you thought so.

3. to ask whether you could kindly help in the matter of sailings from Pembroke Dock to Cork!

I want to go to Cape Clear, Cork towards the end of August and believe it may be cheaper to go from Pembroke Dock rather than via Caergybi and Dublin. The boat used to sail from Abergwaun, was then switched to Abertawe, but now goes from Pembroke Dock to Cork. The trouble is I haven't a clue as to whom to write for information. I foresee a letter addressed to British + Irish Steampacket Co., Pembroke Dock, as likely to return to sender. As you live somewhere in the area, I wondered if you would be very kind and <u>either</u> find out their correct address so that I can contact them, <u>or</u> extract from them a timetable with sailings and fares.

I hope life goes suaviter for you and that you are still finding the time to write.

Cofion cynnes,

Ronald

99

Dear Raymond,

Many thanks for being so kind. It looks definitely cheaper to go that way.

I enclose a brochure about Enlli.

I would be quite willing to come and give a reading at my own expense, taking advantage of your hospitality, providing it was clear that it was all for Ynys Enlli. At an executive meeting yesterday it was pointed out by the solicitor that all money raised for the Appeal must go solely for the purchase of the Island owing to mortgage difficulties etc. Only when the buying price of £103,000 has been passed, can we divert cash for the upkeep, repairs etc. This naturally leaves us short. Apparently (in confidence) there is nothing to stop individuals like myself giving a poetry reading, for instance, 'For Bardsey'. I can then pass that money to the Management Committee to pay for building materials etc. Just a matter of wording and not leading the audience into thinking that my reading is a part of the official Appeal to buy Bardsey, of which there is a special Welsh sub-committee. The notice of my reading would be something like 'Poetry reading by RST. Proceeds in aid of Ynys Enlli / Bardsey Island'. No mention of the Trust, whatever you do! Let me know of possible dates and I'll see if they fit in.

I hope you are not redundant academically. You will never be in other ways.

I hope the Ted Hughes meeting goes well. He is my favourite reader of poetry.

Y Rhiw is 4 miles E.N.E. of Aberdaron. This cottage overlooks Porth Neigwl.

Cofion cynnes,

Ronald

100

Sarn-y-Plas • Y Rhiw • Pwllheli
12.v.78

Dear Raymond,

Many thanks for your letter. It seems unlikely, therefore, that the reading will materialise. I shall be in Ireland until near the end of October and will be committed on my return for the first half of November. It is kind of you to offer a stopping-off place, but as I shall not have the car it looks as if it will be easier to travel between here and Abertawe rather than wandering off into the wilds of 'West Wales' with all my luggage.

I'm glad that Iestyn and Angharad are making good progress.

Cofion,

Ronald

101

Dear Raymond,

Many thanks for yours. I would be free after the middle of November, if you have a Wednesday or Thursday, although I would have to know fairly soon, as there is a Scottish visit being negotiated sometime then as well.

I have rather dropped out of Welsh news since coming here, whilst conducting my own private campaigning against too much English. I don't think any of the 'bodies' are genuinely pro-Welsh, whatever they say publicly.

Regards,

Ronald

102

Y Rhiw
15.vi.78

Dear Raymond,

Many thanks for your letter of 13th received today 15th. It is good of you to help by hiring the hall personally. You should be reimbursed out of the proceeds. We can settle that later. Shall we say Thursday Nov. 23? However 22nd would do, if you felt it was a better night. A good idea to have a display week. Let me know if more brochures are required. We are having difficulty in getting the Welsh Appeal going for lack of a Welsh-speaking secretary. A competent Anglo-Welshwoman is ready and eager, but it is felt by Bedwyr and the Archbishop, rightly, that we should have a Welsh speaker. So we don't move. So typical of the position in Wales. All this pressure and criticism, but so little positive help.

Glad you will soon have Angharad's company.

Ronald

103

Thank you for your letter etc. I have been on an Arts Council tour in East Anglia. I shall hope to reach you about 4.30 pm on Thursday 23rd and will be glad of a bed for the night. I don't know how much literature D.T. has acquired. I could bring some pamphlets etc.

Cofion,

Ronald

104

Dear Raymond,

Just a word of thanks for your hospitality during my brief but pleasant village [*sic*]. I turned aside to Llanpumsaint in an attempt to look at the East window Elsie did years ago. The church was locked, I failed to get an answer at any of the hideous houses, it was like a village of the dead. Then suddenly a herd of cows appeared with four men and dogs. The cows stampeded, the dogs barked, the men shouted in Welsh and a resurrection of a sort occurred. I called on Geraint Bowen, too, but he was out. His wife told me he is giving up editing Y Faner from pressure of other work. Such a shame. But, there we are. I haven't heard yet what happened at Caerfyrddin court.

Cofion,

Ronald

P.S. The lad I introduced – Jonathan Gower – from Pwll, is a good lad.

105

Sarn-y-Plas • Y Rhiw • Pwllheli
19.xii.78

Dear Raymond,

Just a word of greetings. I am so glad you will probably have Angharad to share Christmas with. It is at least peaceful out here. Town Christmases get more like a fair every year. One stationers in Pwllheli has a special box marked: Religious Christmas Cards – which is a nice thought.

Let me commend to your notice TENEBRAE, Geoffrey Hill's new book from André Deutsch. He is a fine poet, certainly the best now writing in English. I wish I wrote with his economy and intelligence. And he is only 46, so there must be much good work to come.

The Ynys Enlli fund grows steadily. I believe we are not far off paying for it. So we can start putting cash by to endow it.

Gyda dymuniadau cu,

R.S.T.

106

Sarn-y-Plas • Y Rhiw • Pwllheli
13.xii.79

My dear Raymond,

Greetings once more at Christmas. It was good to see you in October with Iestyn and Angharad at hand for company.

I have had some sort of malaise lately: a nervous reaction or something which has given me to much thought. Whenever I am unwell I fall to questioning various postures and tenets too easily and arrogantly held when one is well, both in one's life and in poetry. I am writing like this to you because of the difficulty both of us are having with our allegiance to a church which seems to be abandoning too lightly the wonderful traditions which have sustained over the centuries. Many systems and structures tempt one from time to time, but I find, when I am unwell and nervously shaken, that I can't live by them. I can't bring myself to agree that Christianity is the only way, as so many dogmatists claim, but it is certainly one of the great ways and for one brought up in the European tradition, there is little point in turning to one of the other ways. So I am content to leave in such a mysterious and wonderful universe the issues in God's hands, asking pardon for wilfulness and grace for humble trust and acceptance. The church is imperfect, God knows, but it has the scriptures and sacraments, if it only will have the grace to let those who prefer the old forms continue to enjoy them. So I shall still go along on Christmas morning. Perhaps you will?

Cofion cu,

Ronald

107

Dear Raymond,

Things seem to get worse with every Christmas letter I write you, though I try to disregard the ancestral voices prophesying war. The one hopeful feature is the way some of the young ones have seen the light, but the apathy and Philistinism of Llŷn are beyond imagining. Another wraith I engage with is that Christianity is otherworldly. It seems almost incontrovertible. I wish I could have met some of those brave spirits like Bonhoeffer who seem able to live eternity in the moment in the midst of bestiality and woe.

A neighbouring vicar was here yesterday asking me to give a Lenten talk. Enid Pierce Roberts on March 1st on Dewi Sant. And I on the 8th. What would my title be? Ar ôl Dewi, I said.

I hope you as I may have strength and patience to endure in this post Davidum wilderness.

Ronald

108

Dear Raymond,

I'm sorry our paths have not crossed this year. My only visit south was to read with some zany Canadian called Al Purdy in October.

I hope you are well. Will you be able to retire before being made redundant; or does this fate not await you? We worry about Gwydion. How about Angharad? With costs rising, I have been falling back on this area, and cultivating local Welsh contacts, although my age is against me. We have formed a Dwyfor branch of Yr Ymgyrch Gwrth-Nuclear. The apathy and willed ignorance of this area are extreme, but are beginning to crack here and there. I have taken heart a little about the language. Since I no longer move in and out among my parishioners, I am having to push my way in here and there locally, and it is heartening to find pockets of 'good' Welsh people, and to tune my ear to Llŷn Welsh, which is still fluent and natural and to some extent idiomatic, if adulterated with the occasional unnecessary English word.

I hope you are finding the heart to write, even though the market for poetry seems to be drying up, and the critical situation is appalling. What are young people to think when Mr X is hailed by one section as a new major talent, and dismissed by another as a very bad poet indeed?

Anyway forget it and enjoy peace at Christmas.

Cofion cu,

Ronald

109

Dear Raymond,

I was distressed to hear about your arthritis and that you were not feeling like writing. You have had a raw deal one way and another, although I am glad that you get some consolation from teaching. There is, God knows, a need for fearless and committed teaching. I get occasional letters complaining that the writer does not know what to believe, when he is told that so and so is a major poet or a great writer. English criticism is a morass and is made worse by certain dons, who should know better, who delight in saying stupid and irresponsible things in public, e.g. John Carey, Merton Professor of English at Oxford: 'Everybody knows by now that Seamus Heaney is a major poet'. Etc. ad nauseam.

We offset this in Wales by niggling at the one writer of stature (S.L.) and whistling to keep our courage up over the rest.

Eheu, fugaces.

Sincerely,

Ronald

110

Y Rhiw • Pwllheli
16.xii.82

Dear Raymond,

Time for another Christmas letter. This is something still in store for you, the way time flows by. I have now reached the state when I don't know whether it was last year, or the year before, or the year before that, when something happened. When did I eat a lunch with you? I believe it was 3 years ago. I hope you and Iestyn and Angharad are well; your arthritis not getting worse, I hope. It's nice to see Iestyn's name from time to time; and a photo of him in Y Faner a few weeks back. I thought I might have seen you at Llanidloes 3 weeks or so ago, but it's easy to miss people in a crowd. What a shameful business! Angharad Thomas asked me to write to the English press. I sent to The Guardian, Western Mail, Liverpool Post and New Statesman, but as I told her, I didn't expect them to appear. I used to sign letters for Alwyn Rees to papers like The Times, but I don't think they were ever published.

Are you writing? I hope so. I shall be a septuagenarian next March, so Macmillan are bringing out a selection of later poems to balance the earlier selection. I wish they were in Welsh. Awake in bed at night, I try to get back to sleep by composing englynion. I generally get back to sleep, but without the englyn! I don't know how. Yr hen Saesneg diawledig yn yr isymwybod.

I hope you have company at Christmas.

As always,

Ronald

111

Dear Raymond,

It was kind and generous of you to write as you did and I am indeed grateful. The only snag is that I honestly don't recognise myself in the portrait you have drawn.

There is certainly no feeling of achievement at all, but rather of a falling short of what I would have wished to achieve. The sort of yard-sticks I have used have been Bateau Ivre, Le Cimetière Marin, Sailing to Byzantium, Gerontion etc. And when one falls short of those, one knows one hasn't been chosen.

They have fixed this reception in Caerdydd for May 17th. All being well, I think I'll do a 'progress' afterward and visit some of my friends. It would be nice to see you.

I am writing this while still in my sixties! Tuesday is the fatal day.

Cofion,

Ronald

112

Y Rhiw • Pwllheli • Gwynedd
10.v.83

Dear Raymond,

I don't know what your plans are next Tuesday/Wednesday, but following your kind offer I would like to stay with you Wednesday night, if you have not planned otherwise – and I mean the 'if'. Don't bother making up a bed, as I shall have my own sheets + pillow case. I find this saves a bit of bother to my friends these days.

I remember your saying you found public transport more comfortable than private cars. Otherwise you could travel with me on Wednesday afternoon.

Yours sincerely,

Ronald

113

Y Rhiw • Pwllheli
23.v.83

Dear Raymond,

It was good to have talk again, and thank you for your hospitality, also, once again, for coming to Caerdydd.

I gave your regards to the Elisiaid whom I found well.

Cofion,

Ronald

114

Y Rhiw • Pwllheli
31.x.83

Dear Raymond,

Thank you for your letter. I have had a tussle with one or two anthologists who were determined to leave out my later work. Whilst realising that you and Roland Mathias are not of that opinion, I could not avoid the impression which Mike Felton's letter with its list gave – 10 of the earlier poems with 4 later ones tagged on at the end. However, if you will indicate in your introduction, as clearly as in your letter, the principles on which the anthology was compiled, I will give way.

Yours sincerely,

Ronald

115

Y Rhiw • Pwllheli
16.xi.83

Dear Raymond,

Thank you for your two letters and enclosures. I don't agree with you, of course, whilst sympathising with your aims. In view of your rather Politburo views, I shall proceed happily as a deviationist, periodically going through my m/s and consigning to the waste basket what I am not satisfied that the public should see.

The Llŷn ac Eifionydd CND are going by 'bus to Caerdydd on Dec. 3rd, but as we have to leave at 4/30 a.m., I don't know whether I shall be awake enough to walk in procession.

Yn bur,

Ronald

116

Y Rhiw • Pwllheli • Gwynedd
17.xii.83

Dear Raymond,

My Christmas greetings to you once again, although internationally things have hardly improved since last time. America seems to be taking over everything. The Cambridge Poetry Magazine asked me for a poem, but I notice their first number was given over entirely to American poets.

I was down in Cardiff on Dec. 3rd, but was disappointed there were not more protesters. We thought of hiring a bus, but because of lack of numbers, went in private cars. This meant leaving here at 5.0 a.m.

I have just been reading in London with a Norwegian poet. As Fraser Steel kindly put it: 'He's even older than you are'. So we made a good pair. Poetry readings have a mystique which I can't fathom. We stayed with Gwydion in his new, little house in Kew. Oh, dear – English suburban life! But what to do? That's where his work is. Let us at least rejoice that you and I live yng Nghymru.

Cofion cu,

Ronald

117

Y Rhiw • Pwllheli • Gwynedd
31.vii.84

Dear Raymond,

It was good to hear from you, and that Iestyn has Gwynfor's house. Mutual satisfaction, surely. We have our Llŷn ac Eifionydd CND exhibition on this week. We do not make much headway. Llŷn is bulging at the seams now. I feel so sorry for the not-too-bright shop assistants turning or trying to from one language to the other. I have been experiencing some of their peevishness lately since my unwillingness to kowtow is beginning to get known. It seems that Llŷn is a place designed by God for the English to have a good time in, and woe betide anyone who suggests that perhaps it was where he wanted Welshmen to be themselves. I do so admire young women like Angharad Tomos, who go bravely on campaigning for what they believe in.

Yn bur,

Ronald

118

Y Rhiw • Pwllheli
6.x.84

Dear Raymond,

Thank you for your letter. Yes, Elsie fell in the road and broke her thigh bone. She has been home about 12 days and is recovering, although this cottage is all steps. The arteritis she suffered in Aberdaron left her weak in the legs and this coupled with sight in one eye only makes her balance unstable.

I'm glad you are able to get over to Llangadog when you want to.

I had an invitation to the Conference in Caerdydd on Nov. 3rd about a new law for the Welsh language.

I don't [know] whether I shall see you there? I shall have to go, far as it is.

Cofion,

Ronald

119

Y Rhiw
16.xii.84

Dear Raymond,

Thank you for your letter and greetings. Elsie is coming along with the aid of the metal 'pulpit'.

At the meeting in Caerdydd, although Gwilym Bangor, as chairman, asked all non-Welsh speakers to make sure their translation receivers were working so that proceedings could go smoothly in Welsh, John Morris, after 2 or 3 minutes of preliminary Welsh, spent the rest of his address in speaking English. It sounded so much more impressive in English for him to tell us what he did when he was Secretary of State. I would have walked out, but like many another, no doubt, did not want to jeopardise any chances of success. However, people like him will, doubtless, see to it that the effort turns into a damp squib.

I can't forgive the miners for their lack of interest in Welsh. There they are in a Welsh town like Caernarfon with their stall and collecting appeals entirely in English.

I have always blamed them for setting the class struggle before the national one. If they had identified with the Welsh cause instead of the workers in England and the Labour party, we would have self-government by now. They are indignant at police treatment, but they didn't care a damn how the police treated Cymdeithas yr Iaith.

Have a happy day.

Ronald

120

Rhagfyr [December] 1985

Dear Raymond,

Greetings once again. I hope your condition has not deteriorated greatly and that you will be going to Llangadog at Christmas. I saw the sign when I was on my way to Abertawe recently to give the J.R. Jones memorial lecture. How these Welsh towns appal. One might as well be visiting Leicester or Nottingham – the acquisitive crowds pouring their cash into the pockets of the manufacturers of trash, before rushing home to gawp at the television. I saw nature becoming more and more domesticated, while the towns grow more and more violent.

I still rush about over CND matters, achieving little.

I have started a Society here – Cyfeillion Llŷn – as an effort to save something of Llŷn Welshness, and to offset the English influx. New English families arrive here monthly with kids to cancel the Welsh majority in the primary schools. Gloomy thoughts of an old man – but not in a dry season. It rains and rains.

Kind thoughts nevertheless,

Ronald

121

Dear Raymond,

Thank you for your kind letter. I have been down in Caerfyrddin twice within the last 2 months over the Bunker business without a chance to see you. The reason the first time was I came with others and was dependent on them. The second, last Tuesday morning, was that I had four others in the car with me and they were dependent on me. We were at Breudeth on the Monday, and I stayed the night with Gwynfor while the others stayed with Guto Prys. The whole business is unspeakable. Trawsfynydd are arranging a series of junketings to celebrate their 21st birthday. Are the Welsh boycotting? Not on your life.

Cofion caredig,

Ronald

122

Y Rhiw • Pwllheli
[Christmas 1986]

Dear Raymond,

Let me begin with an invitation to join my secret army. There is no membership fee, and arms of all kinds can be obtained from any industrialised country. You have to pay for those, naturally. I often think of your description of the imperialist heroes as butchers.

I hope your arthritis is under some sort of control. There are pain clinics, I understand. But I expect you know about them.

I stayed a night with Gwynfor last summer after a CND rally and we spoke of Iestyn's occupation of Y Dalar Wen. Gwynfor has called his new home by the same name, as you know.

I was down in Cernyw in October, a gloomy foretaste of what could happen to us, indeed has happened in Gwent, parts of Powys, Dyfed, Morgannwg, Clwyd and is fast happening here under immigration. My society 'Cyfeillion Llŷn' is a forlorn effort to stop the rot here.

In the circumstances I wish you a not too uncomfortable Christmas.

Ronald

123

Y Rhiw • Pwllheli
[Christmas 1987]

Dear Raymond,

Christmas greetings in the hope that you are not too crippled to get to Llangadog for it. I was glad to see Gwasg Gomer had made some reparation to you in publishing your selection.

I imagine you were high enough up at Glannant not to be threatened by the floods. I was up in Northumberland at the time, but nothing happened there, and I was glad to find things all right here on my return. I expect I told you about 'Cyfeillion Llŷn', the movement we started 2 years ago to try to do something here. We go along slowly without startling success, but our existence is recognised! I have also got drawn into CADNO, the movement to oppose a P.W.R. at Trawsfynydd. The district, of course, is split, which is as the Tories desire.

I wonder how your writing life goes along. I addressed, under pressure from H. Pritchard Jones, a meeting of the Union of Welsh Writers in Harlech in September. I didn't enjoy it, neither, I imagine, did they. I have little sympathy with the 'Good a Welshman as you, mun' attitude of the south.

Cofion cynnes,

Ronald

124

Y Rhiw • Pwllheli
5.iii.88

Dear Raymond,

I have had a letter from Belinda Humfrey asking for something for the New Welsh Review (bondigrybwyll). I don't feel disposed to contribute to something which displaces the Anglo-Welsh one with the Arts Council's blessing, as I suspect shady dealings somewhere; but out here, I don't know what goes on in Committees and lobbies. I thought I would sound you before replying.

I don't know if you saw my performance on Byd ar Bedwar recently. I didn't, but I hear from friends that my 2 main points were omitted as 'inflammatory'. They were (1) that property is of far less value than life and (2) that even if one Englishman got killed, what is that compared with the killing of our nation?

Cofion caredig,

Ronald

125

Y Rhiw • Pwllheli
16.iii.88

Dear Raymond,

Thank you for your letter and its enclosure. I told Belinda Humfrey that I hadn't anything at present. I hope you have a safe and enjoyable journey around the eastern Mediterranean.

Cofion,

Ronald

126

Y Rhiw • Pwllheli
27.v.88

Dear Raymond,

Thank you for your letter. It reminded me I had not yet thanked you for your card from Greece. It was kind of you to think of me out there. I am glad, too, of the good news of Angharad.

You must know what I am trying to do in Wales. While I was a priest I tried to promote peace in my parishes in the name of the prince of peace. Through the difficult years of war I never prayed for victory etc. as I was expected to do. My interpretation of Jesus was that he was a pacifist. *He was not.*

What have we in Wales to-day? A hypocritical nation that pretends it is against violence, but acquiesces in it at England's bidding, even derives a vicarious thrill from waving Union Jacks to welcome her victorious heroes from unnecessary capers such as the Malvinas. When England feels herself threatened the call goes out to her people to fight and to give their lives. When Wales is threatened – oh, no. Hide behind a mountain of ignorance, cowardice and double-talk. I want to waken Wales to put aside her servility and humbug.

Cofion,

Ronald

127

Y Rhiw • Pwllheli • Gwynedd
7.vi.88

Dear Raymond,

The morning after the latest extension of the campaign to warn England and draw attention to an injustice by pushing a few more devices through the letter-boxes of estate agents. I was telephoned for my reaction by Dylan Iorwerth. It was news to me, but I said, as you know, and knowing as we all know, that these people, if caught, will be subjected to very heavy sentences by the bought judiciary, that I admired their courage. I don't see a close connection between this and your long condemnation of violence against the person.

Cofion,

Ronald

128

Y Rhiw • Pwllheli
5.viii.88

Dear Raymond,

I appreciated your kind remarks, although I was a bit surprised. Most of the poems had been making a nuisance of themselves in odd corners, so rather than pitch them out, I strung them on a length of prose and offered them to Macmillan, half expecting them to decline.

[. . .]

Cofion caredig,

Ronald

129

Y Rhiw • Pwllheli
[Christmas 1988]

Dear Raymond,

I hope all is well and the grandchild flourishing. How is your arthritis? I have all sorts of aches, which could be anything. An enforced pacifist! I would be no good in a scuffle anymore, so I go round in the dark burning English houses! I wonder if Peter Walker and his sycophants have any idea of what it is like in Llŷn. A tiny cottage near Botwnnog that was partially burned a few years ago has had a new, larger bungalow built on the site, which is on offer by the English owner at £85,000! Is it any wonder the young people of Llŷn live in caravans?

I wonder how you spend your time. Doing some writing, I hope.

I was down with the Merriman Society in Caerdydd in June and raised my glass to Cathleen ni Houlihan. It was vigorously responded to. Elin ap Hywel's translation into Welsh of The Midnight Court sounded well.

Nadolig dedwydd,

Ronald

130

Y Rhiw • Pwllheli
1.vii.89

Dear Raymond,

Once again it was kind of you to remember me on your travels. I hope you enjoyed it all and were not too hindered by arthritis. I wonder what the original Troy was 'really' like? And Helen? Llywelyn's castle at Dolwyddelan is such a small affair.

Kind wishes,

Ronald

131

Dear Raymond,

Thank you for your interesting letter and the photographs. I'm glad you enjoyed your visit. I hope your ascent of Parnassus kindles some poetry in you. [. . .]

It amuses me to make odd poems on some of the cards people send me. Here is my effort on the first you sent of Troy.

Yours sincerely,

Ronald

*   *   *

A notice to inform
the unlettered: This is Troy.
And the dust whispering:
My kiss was the prize
for which warriors contended.

We admire the view which
for ten years they ignored.
What runners they were,
round and round the arena
in their expensive armour!

Like that other runner
from Marathon, his time
unsurpassed until the arrival
of steroids. We cover the ground
faster, but what news do we bring?

132

Y Rhiw
[Christmas 1989]

Dear Raymond,

I don't know where you will be this Christmas, but wherever you are, I hope you will be as happy as may be in this disturbed world, that creates problems as fast as it solves them. One welcomes the outbursts in Europe, although it makes one ashamed that we Welsh are so supine. The disturbing aspect is that the patent brutalities and stupidities of the Communist world are leading to the self-congratulation of the capitalist one. But one can't ignore the fact that there are more nationally conscious elements in countries like Hungary and Czechoslovakia, as well as more politically informed ones, than we can boast of yng Nghymru. Who have we to compare with Saunders and Alwyn Rees? And England has been canny enough to sugar the pill of anglicisation.

We have our monthly committee of Cyfeillion Llŷn tonight, a body of well-disposed worthies of Llŷn, but without teeth, and not over-disturbed by the fact. As Secretary, I have written scores of letters and attended dozens of protests, without much visible effect. And yet it is better that we exist, rather than not.

I hope your arthritis is no worse. Elsi is in pretty poor shape really and not improving, I'm afraid.

Cofion caredig,

Ronald

133

Dear Raymond,

Thank you for your letter. I was so glad to hear you were writing poetry again. You sound as if you experienced something of what I did nearly 10 years ago, not all that long after I had breakfasted with you, you remember. I didn't connect the two at the time, but a year or two before I retired we had gone onto a vegetarian diet. I was aware of the dangers and eased off gradually. However, I had been feeling more and more on edge, until suddenly one night something snapped and I was seized with uncontrollable shivers. This was followed by a week of extreme depression, and, as you mention, claustrophobia. The doctor put me on vallium, and I myself returned to meat which I still take to my regret. Elsi, delicate as she is, has tougher nerves, but like me takes meat again. All this, as a point of comparison, but it certainly exposed weaknesses in me. There is a faint line, indeed, between nerves and cowardice, as there is between strong nerves and courage.

Blwyddyn newydd well,

Ronald

134

[Postcard]

17.viii.90

It was kind of you to think of me on your journey. I hope you enjoyed it. You see, Saesneg in Rhuddlan as early as this!

Cofion,

R.S.

135

Dear Raymond,

So the Christmases pass and I begin to have the feeling I have stayed too long. But I must not go yet, because Elsi is in pretty poor shape and needs help.

I hope your arthritis is under control. I am glad to see you are writing again. What a strange world it is now. So many people that one can hardly say anything without its being disproved. I suppose there was always vulgarity and display. Once it was the Pharaohs, the Emperors, the Rajahs; now it is the sportsmen, the show-biz types, the tycoons. 'Let us endure an hour and see injustice done.' I wonder whether you discover any good new poetry. Out here in the bush nothing comes my way.

I hope Iestyn and Angharad flourish and that you will have a worthwhile Christmas.

Yn garedig,

Ronald

136

Y Rhiw • Pwllheli
23.ii.91

Dear Raymond,

Thank you for the splendid photograph of Delphi. Yes, Cymru. Thank God I am still able to see and love it without the media.

Cofion,

Ronald

137

Y Rhiw • Pwllheli
16.iii.91

Dear Raymond,

I have the sad news that Elsi passed away from this world last Sunday, March 10th. She had not enjoyed good health for the last 20 years, but was obviously deteriorating over this last period. She was of great courage and rarely complained. Mercifully the end came quite quickly and she died peacefully.

Gwydion came at once and was a great help over the worst few days. He is going to America at the end of the month, visiting certain universities in the south as representative of Ealing College. Sharon and Rhodri will be going with him, which is good.

I hope all goes well with you three. Your postcard of Delphi was the best view I know.

Cofion,

Ronald

138

Y Rhiw • Pwllheli • Gwynedd
20.iii.91

Dear Raymond,

Many thanks for your kind message and your offer of a bed anytime. I will remember that, if I happen to be in the vicinity.

Cofion cynnes,

R.S.

139

Dear Raymond,

Every Christmas, when I come to write you my seasonal letter, the situation in Wales seems to have deteriorated. There is misery among my patriotic friends here, as they see a nation and its language being destroyed by a hundred and one things, which I hardly need retail to you. And the shame is that Welsh supineness, indifference, materialism and a willingness to be conditioned are almost as much to blame as outside pressures. Not that the world is in much better shape. The materialism of the West is bound to bring nemesis upon it before long. It is disheartening to see how little support green politics command at the polls, while the rest are poisoning the earth to death. 'There's no use complaining for money's rant is on.' What would Yeats say now?

I expect you will be seeing your family at Christmas. I hope you have a happy time and a successful new year.

Ronald

140

Dear Raymond,

Here it has come round again with distressing speed, the time when I should 'pen this missive' as your forefathers would have put it. I hope mine spoke Welsh, but one can't be sure. How did Yeats know his blood had not passed through any huckster's loins? I am glad to see from 'Planet' that you are publishing again.

I did a bit of globe-trotting this year, Poland in May and north Greece in September, both tours in search of birds. The villages and small farmsteads of east Poland reminded me very much of Chekhov. We were at times only a few miles from the Russian border. There is an ancient forest, which is a reserve. The Polish guerrillas used to make sorties against the Germans and then disappear into the trees. The Germans true to type would then victimise the villagers. In Greece we pursued God up Olympos, but he vanished, as always, into thin air.

The burned-up landscape did make me realise how we malign our own climate. We did have one downpour on Olympos. Perhaps God is a monkey after all. They like to urinate at strangers.

Cyfarchion Nadolig,

Ronald

141

Y Rhiw • Pwllheli • Gwynedd
8.iii.93

Dear Raymond,

Thank you for your kind letter. I was born at the end of the month, just missing April Fool's Day. It is ironic that I wrote that poem in Eglwys Fach congratulating the old thing for living so long, and now I am being congratulated. 'I had forgiven enough, that had forgiven old age.'

I am receiving various essays + reviews. I see some people are still nit-picking about my so-called lack of form. I wish they'd catch up. John Wain, one of the Movement bunch, seems to have begun it, and Donald Davie, another Movement fan, agrees, carrying on about 'enjambement' etc., as if that mattered any more. Larkin was the good thing that came out of the Movement. To me form is something much more than the look of the poem on the page. Form is a large subject and needs wider treatment. I haven't come across any, which doesn't mean there isn't.

Cofion cynnes,

Ronald

142

Upper House • Brierley Hill • Presteigne • Powys
11.x.93

Dear Raymond,

Thank you for your letter.

I told the Caerdydd festival I didn't want to bring you all that way.

I'm glad to hear your news.

I have taken this house for 6 months to be near some friends who have problems.

Cofion cynnes,

Ronald

Llanandras is Presteigne, but it causes delay.

143

Upper House • Brierley Hill • Presteigne • Powys
17.xii.93

Dear Raymond,

Christmas greetings from England! I don't remember whether I told you I had taken this house until the end of March to be near some former friends to help them. They came to Eglwys Fach, moved near Tywyn and then over here. Betty Kirk-Owen lived with her small daughter, Alice, and Richard Vernon. [. . .]

I wonder what you think of contemporary English poetry, so-called. I was sent an anthology of Forward poetry recently. I never saw a worse collection of trivia and was appalled to hear a copy of it is being sent to every secondary school in the country. They review and praise each other and win awards for their brilliance. Technology and the media have produced a shallow generation, so poets are praised as its spokesman. Where art the great organ notes of English poetry?

I hope you keep at it.

Ronald

144

Cefn Du Ganol • Llanfairynghornwy • Caergybi • LL65 4LG
13.xii.94

Dear Raymond,

I had not foreseen this move. Across the bay is where I was 'raised', although the school where I was 'educated' was long ago pulled down to make way for a glass complex like any cheap office block. [. . .] How is the arthritis? I'm glad you are writing. What does one make of contemporary 'poetry' in English? The old have always had difficulty in adjusting to the new. But is the present's offering worth adjusting to? Believe it or not I went on an Alaska cruise last July. Betty wanted to see relatives in British Columbia.

I hope Iestyn and Angharad flourish.

Cofion caredig,

Ronald

145

[Cefn Du Ganol • Llanfair-yng-Nghornwy • Caergybi]
19.viii.95

Dear Raymond,

Thank you for your letter. I enclose a suggestion since it is for a disabled colleague of yours. I trust you are well and functioning.

Cofion caredig,

Ronald

*   *   *

Questions to the Prophet

How will the lion remain a lion
if it eat straw like the ox?

Where will the little child lead them
who has not been there before?

With our right hand off, with what
shall we beg forgiveness in the kingdom?

How shall the hare know it has not won,
dying before the tortoise arrive?

Did Christ crying: 'Neither do I condemn thee'
condemn the prostitute to be good for nothing?

If he who increases riches increases sorrow
why are his tears more like pearls than the swine's tusks?

1. R.S. Thomas. Born 1913 in Caerdydd. Ordained into the Church in Wales in 1936. Retired 1978.

2. Influenced by Welsh landscape, history and language and literature, and by as many poets as he was able to read in English, Welsh and French.

3. The poem aims to explore the ironies in the Old and New Testament as well as a paradox of Zeno, the Greek philosopher.

Experience of life teaches that hardly any of the verses in the Bible can be taken at face value. Each of these verses should be looked at carefully with the realisation that profound issues are involved.

For instance there is much sentimentality connected with the idea of childhood; yet true adulthood knows things which are beyond a child's grasp.

Similarly there is a lot of condemnation of wealth, and yet it is the secret desire of the majority of mankind.

So with prostitution. It is not a pleasant idea; yet it is practised world-wide and amongst fallen humanity who can compute the profit and loss?

We know that most of Christ's sayings were metaphorical, yet by taking one such as going into the kingdom without one's right hand literally a new twist can be given it.

146

Dear Raymond,

I'm afraid I am a bit late this Christmas. A visit to Catalunya as part of a Welsh delegation in November was followed by an Arts Council tour to the five cities of Britain, from which I have just returned. I have always avoided Ulster, but took advantage of the so-called ceasefire to visit Belfast. We went there on Sunday, so I don't know whether so many shops were shuttered because of I.R.A. militancy or because of Sabbatarianism. Anyway it seemed a charmless city compared with Dublin. The Irish punt is now stronger than Sterling which makes nonsense of our enemies' arguments that Wales would not be economically viable. However my Irish friends admit that our language is stronger. And Iain Crichton Smith, one of the delegation, was only too well aware, as I am, of the fragility of Gaelic.

'I grow old' but do not wear the bottoms of my trousers rolled. I trust you are well, have good news of the family and will prosper in 1996.

Ronald

147

Llanfairynghornwy • Caergybi • LL65 4LG
8.xi.96

Dear Raymond,

Thank you for your letter.

I appreciate your absenting yourself from Harper Collins' attempt to promote their book. They wrote to me a couple of years ago or more saying they had commissioned Wintle to write my biography. I replied saying I did not want a biography. My reply to Wintle was the same, and when they decided to go ahead regardless, I refused to have anything to do with them. I did reply to Wintle at one stage saying that I had no objection to a study of my work by a competent critic. He took this to mean that I was giving my blessing to his biography! I have been sent a copy of the book, but don't intend reading it. I hear from one or two who have that, as you would expect, it falls between two stools.

I hope your health is not too bad. As at Rhiw, I am far from a good bookshop, so have not seen the book on you. I re-married in August someone I have known for many years, so here we are, two octogenarians trying to ignore the fact.

Cofion caredig,

Ronald

148

[Postcard]

Llanfairynghornwy • Caergybi • LL65 4LG
21.xi.96

I'm in a whiz preparing to go off for 3 weeks, so am late thanking you for your note, much appreciated by us.

Cofion caredig,

Ronald

149

Llanfairynghornwy • Caergybi • LL65 4LG
19.xii.96

Dear Raymond,

Another Christmas! How many more? Betty thinks I am immortal; I leave it to God, fate, destiny – my circulation.

We were out in the U.A.E. the end of November into December. Betty is no birdwatcher, but I thought she might enjoy other aspects. It was not a very successful tour, but she has seen a lot of the world, so it didn't matter all that much. I saw some desert birds and aspects of Arab life. It was strange to see Dubai, a new modern city rising out of the desert. There is plenty of money there and no unemployment. I had to go to Munich on the way back to receive a prize. Thanks to the many poems which Kevin Perryman has translated, the Bavarian Academy decided to give me a prize. I don't take to Germans or their language, but it was kind of them and I treated them to a little Welsh at the ceremony!

I am hoping to retire from air travel now, but who knows? I hope your arthritis is under control and that you will get over to Angharad for Christmas.

Cofion caredig,

Ronald

150

Llanfairynghornwy • Caergybi • LL65 4LG
18.xii.97

Dear Raymond,

I soldier on with an uneasy feeling of having outstayed my welcome, although glad to have seen Siôn Aubrey released. 6 years of a young man's life to give the police an undeserved sense of satisfaction.

I was glad to see a selection of your poems had been published. Was it Gomer trying to make amends? I hope Iestyn and Angharad flourish and that you continue able to visit them.

I recently bought a television set for Betty to have something to look at. As her sight deteriorates, she finds it increasingly difficult to read.

She suffered a major loss in March, when her only daughter, Alice, died at 40. We knew she could not live, but it didn't make it any easier to lose such a vivid and brave person. There have been many interruptions this year, so I have never really got down to much poetry writing. Yet I feel this in itself is a kind of excuse, because the lyrical spring is running dry at last. I was lucky it ran for so long. I believe you went on Swan Hellenic cruises. We went in November. Betty visited Jerusalem. I wouldn't go. We gawped at the pyramids. I was in Luxor two days before the massacre.

With best wishes for Christmas,

Ronald

151

Tŷ Main • Llanfrothen • Gwynedd • LL48 6SG
16.xii.98

Annwyl Raymond,

We left Ynys Môn in April and are now entered on our first year on the Meirionnydd border between Eifionydd and Ardudwy, one of the scenic gems of Wales – we step out of our door and see Yr Wyddfa in front of us. The district is also about 85% Welsh-speaking. We also have a traditional cottage. We are more central here strangely with the railway station at Penrhyndeudraeth only 2 miles away. We thought we were wise in providing against old age, but hadn't realised what it would be like living in too small a house – there is only one bedroom. However we must adapt. A splendid woman 'does' for us 4 days a week and is always ready to help in emergencies. Thus our history. What of you? I hope the arthritis is kept at bay and that you still write. Owing to 6 months' turmoil I have had little repose and feel I will never write anything significant again – at 85 the one enemy is repetition. I suppose it is age, too, which precludes my seeing much worth in most of the young poets in English to-day. I hope you enjoy Christmas and that all is well with Iestyn + Angharad.

Cofion cynnes,

Ronald

152

Twll y Cae • Pentrefelin • Cricieth • LL52 OPU
17.xii.99

Dear Raymond,

Here we are yet again moved, I hope, for the last time. The house in Llanfrothen was far too small. I hope you are comfortable. I expect you, as I, take a long view of the Millennium. As if 5 minutes before and 5 after can make any difference.

My heart has begun misbehaving, which means I can no longer hurry or go for long walks. And since I am full of tablets, I go to sleep at the drop of a hat, which means I am unlikely to write any more poetry. I hope you haven't reached that stage of senility. Yeats was railing against it at a much younger age. I hope you still find pleasure in your children. [. . .] I am unlikely to journey south again. You would be very welcome, if you found yourself up here.

Greetings,

Ronald

NOTES AND REFERENCES

Translations of Welsh valedictions at the end of letters, and a glossary of Welsh place-names mentioned in the text, are given at the end of this section.

Abbreviations: RST = R.S. Thomas; RG = Raymond Garlick

p. 3 your discussion on the radio: 'Literary Notebook: What is Anglo-Welsh Literature?', broadcast 3 June 1951 on the BBC Welsh Home Service. The speakers were RG, Roland Mathias, Glyn Jones and Howard Sergeant, and the discussion was chaired by A.G. Prys-Jones. RG's many contributions to radio had started as far back as 1946 when he was an undergraduate at Bangor (see the Introduction). On his broadcasts during the 1950s, see RG's 'Dylan Thomas and Others', *Planet*, 109 (February/March 1995), 81–82.

p. 3 your magazine: *Dock Leaves*, founded in 1949. One of its aims was to bridge the language divide in literary Wales. Since 1949, RG had been a teacher at Pembroke Dock County School. As a member of a south-Pembrokeshire literary discussion society (the 'Dock Leaves Group'), he was one of the magazine's main founders and its first editor (1949–60). In 1957 RG changed the title to *The Anglo-Welsh Review*. Its editor 1961–76 was Roland Mathias, 1976–84 Gillian Clarke, and 1984–88 Greg Hill.

p. 4 10.vii.51: superinscribed on this letter is RG's comment: 'The original of this, RST's second letter to me, is framed & hangs on my wall'.

p. 4 the enclosed poem: 'Depopulation of the Hills' was published in *Dock Leaves* 2, 6 (Michaelmas 1951), 23.

p. 4 a limited edition of poems: *An Acre of Land* (Newtown: Montgomeryshire Printing Co., 1952).

p. 6 my last [i.e. latest] book: *An Acre of Land.* See also note on **P.S. Thank you for reviewing mine**, p. 161 below.

p. 7 Miss Crocker: Miss Beatrice Crocker, English teacher at Holyhead County School, 1919–46.

p. 7 hearing your talk on Saturday: 'On Going South', broadcast 26 January 1952 on the BBC Welsh Home Service. RG's talk was an account of a journey through France to Spain, and included a vivid description of the pilgrims visiting the shrine at Lourdes, together with a portrait of the city of Madrid.

p. 7 I would like to visit Spain: mainly for bird-watching. RST's subsequent visits to Ireland, Poland, Greece, the United Arab Emirates and Scandinavia were also ornithological trips. A visit to Spain (to the Coto Doñana nature reserve on the south-west coast) came about in 1966, in the company of his friend, the distinguished naturalist William Condry (1918–98); see Jason Walford Davies (ed. and trans.), *R.S. Thomas: Autobiographies* (London: J.M. Dent, 1997), 68–70, and the poems 'No, Señor', 'Coto Doñana' and 'Burgos' in *Not That He Brought Flowers* (1968).

p. 8 I shall be off to London . . . to be cured of my extreme nationalism!: an ironic gloss on the BBC radio programme *The Critics*, which had discussed Thomas's *An Acre of Land*. As Raymond Garlick recalled in his Editorial in *Dock Leaves*, 6, 18 (Winter 1955), 2: 'Although the publicity given to *An Acre of Land* in the BBC programme *The Critics* helped to sell out the book when it was first published, those who heard this broadcast will recall that the Welshness – not merely in subject, but in allegiance – of the poems stuck in the throats of some of those who discussed them: until Mr. Alan Pryce-Jones [then editor of the *Times Literary Supplement*] succeeded somewhat in broadening their minds. R.S. Thomas's poetry is written without reference or deference to London, and some of *The Critics* appeared to find this irreverent'.

p. 8 'gnawing the carcase': an allusion to RST poems in *An Acre of Land*: 'Worrying the carcase of an old song' ('Welsh Landscape'), 'Gnawing the skin from the small bones' ('The Welsh Hill Country'), 'gnawing the bones/ Of a dead culture' ('Welsh History').

p. 8 'ni bydd diwedd byth ar sŵn y delyn aur': correctly, 'ni cheir diwedd/ Byth ar sŵn y delyn aur' ('there will never be an end to the sound of the golden harp'), from 'Dechrau Canu, Dechrau Canmol' ('A Start to Singing, A Start to Praising'), a famous hymn by William Williams Pantycelyn (1717–91). The lines refer to the rejoicing of the 'pilgrims' in heaven. RST included the quotation in the final section of his poem 'Border Blues', first published in *Dock Leaves*, 4, 11 (Summer 1953), 8–11, and subsequently collected in *Poetry for Supper* (1958).

p. 9 Mr Mathias' book: RST reviewed Roland Mathias's *The Roses of Tretower* (Pembroke Dock: Dock Leaves Press, 1952) in *Dock Leaves*, 3, 8 (Summer 1952), 34–35.

p. 9 P.S. Thank you for reviewing mine: RST's *An Acre of Land* was reviewed by RG in *Dock Leaves* 3, 7 (Spring 1952), 46–49.

p. 10 Annwyl Gyfeillion: this, the only letter written completely in Welsh, translates as follows:

> Dear Friends,
> It was truly kind of you to welcome me in your happy home in Pembrokeshire. Much thanks.
> I returned safely on Friday night, but I had to go away again yesterday.
> I saw the old friend D.J. in Fishguard and had an interesting conversation and a welcome from Mrs Williams – and then, on with my journey through Aberystwyth to Manafon.
> Sincerely,
> R.S. Thomas

RST had visited RG at his house in Argyle St., Pembroke Dock – their first meeting.

p. 10 yr hen gyfaill D.J.: 'the old friend D.J.' – David John Williams (1885–1970), one of Wales's finest prose writers, noted especially for his autobiographical works and short stories. He was one of the early members of Plaid Genedlaethol Cymru, (later Plaid Cymru/The Party of Wales). In 1936, with Saunders Lewis (1893–1985) and Lewis Valentine (1893–1986), he set fire to buildings at the Penyberth bombing school, Llŷn, a symbolic act of arson for which he was imprisoned for nine months in Wormwood Scrubs.

p. 11 Mathias' poems: see note on **Mr Mathias' book** above.

p. 11 the Tourist poem: 'To the Tourist', *Dock Leaves* 3, 8 (Summer 1952), 4 (published in *Song at the Year's Turning* (1955), with small changes, as 'A Welshman to Any Tourist').

p. 12 'Y Faner': *Baner ac Amserau Cymru* ('The Banner and Times of Wales'), originally an influential weekly newspaper established in 1859. In 1977 it became a weekly magazine, publishing numerous letters and several important prose pieces by RST. It ceased publication in 1992.

p. 12 Mathias' book . . . a sort of Welsh rendering: RST's review in Welsh of Roland Mathias's *The Roses of Tretower* appeared under the title 'Cerddi Cymro Di-Gymraeg' ('The Poems of a Non-Welsh-Speaking Welshman') in *Y Faner*, 2 July 1952, 7.

p. 12 the word 'pash' in rereading Hopkins: in his review of Roland Mathias's *The Roses of Tretower* (see note on **Mr Mathias' book**, p. 161 above), RST had complained, 'I do not know the word "pashing" [in Mathias's 'Coed Anghred'] . . . or is this a misprint?'. He had obviously subsequently come across the word in Hopkins's 'Spelt from Sibyl's Leaves': 'self ín self stéepèd and páshed'. Pash: 'to dash (a thing) in pieces; to smash by blows . . . to strike violently' (OED).

p. 12 your radio ode: 'Requiem for a Poet', an elegy for the young Welsh poet R. Aled Hughes. The poem was commissioned by the BBC for a series of 'Radio Odes', and broadcast from Cardiff on the Welsh Home Service on 26 June 1952 (it was subsequently rebroadcast by Radio Éireann from Dublin); later published as *Requiem for a Poet* (Pembroke Dock: Dock Leaves Press, [1953] (Dock Leaves Pamphlet No. 1)).

p. 13 my 'pryddest': a *pryddest* in Welsh is a long poem in free metre. *The Minister*, a poem for four voices in the 'Radio Odes' series, was first broadcast on the BBC Welsh Home Service on 18 September 1952, later printed independently (1953), and subsequently included in *Song at the Year's Turning* (1955). See also note on **'The Minister' is going to be done on the 3rd Program**, p. 168 below.

p. 13 I don't think I shall be at Pencader: Gwynfor Evans (1912–2005, President of Plaid Cymru 1945–81, MP for Carmarthen 1966–70 and 1974–79 – Plaid Cymru's first ever MP) had arranged a large rally for the end of September 1952 at Pencader in Carmarthenshire. The highlight of the occasion was the unveiling of a memorial stone, brought from the Caernarfonshire village of Trefor, commemorating 'Hen Ŵr Pencader' (The Old Man of Pencader). Giraldus Cambrensis (Gerald of Wales, *c.*1146–1223) in his *Descriptio Kambriae* (1194) tells how The Old Man answered Henry II's question as to what would be Wales's fate in the face of England's military might by saying that it would 'never be totally destroyed by the wrath of man, unless at the same time it is punished by the wrath of God', and adding: 'I do not think that on the Day of Direst Judgement any race other than the Welsh, or any other language, will give answer to the Supreme Judge of all for this small corner of the earth'; see

Gerald of Wales, *The Journey Through Wales/The Description of Wales*, trans. Lewis Thorpe (Harmondsworth: Penguin Books, 1978), 274. RST's 'The Tree' (from *An Acre of Land*) was included in a pamphlet of poems published to mark the occasion of the rally; see *Pencader Poems* (Cardiff: Plaid Cymru, 1952), n.p.

p. 14 The Minister: see note on **my 'pryddest'**, p. 162 above. The 'Radio Ode' was published by the Montgomeryshire Printing Co., Newtown, in 1953.

p. 14 Nadolig bendigedig i chwi eich dau: 'A wonderful Christmas to you both'.

p. 14 your reviews last night . . . 5 minutes for Dylan Thomas' Collected Poems!: 'Welsh Bookshelf: A Review of Books by Welsh Authors', broadcast 19 December 1952 on the BBC Welsh Home Service. In addition to Dylan Thomas's *Collected Poems*, RG also discussed D. Parry-Jones's *Welsh Country Characters* and David Jones's *The Anathémata*. RG's review of the latter was published in *Dock Leaves*, 3, 10 (Spring 1953), 44–46.

p. 14 Hopkins: the poet-priest Gerard Manley Hopkins (1844–89) received Welsh lessons from a Miss Susannah Jones, who lived close to St Beuno's College in the Vale of Clwyd where, between 1874 and 1877, Hopkins completed his training for the Jesuit priesthood. Several aspects of strict-metre verse in the Welsh language profoundly influenced Hopkins's poetry.

p. 15 your poem: *Requiem for a Poet* (Pembroke Dock: Dock Leaves Press, [1953] (Dock Leaves Pamphlet No. 1)); see note on **your radio ode**, p. 162 above.

p. 15 my renewal subscription: to *Dock Leaves*.

p. 15 a sermon on it – The adoption: in 1952 RG and his wife Elin (née Hughes) adopted a son, Iestyn. In 1958 they were to adopt a daughter, Angharad.

p. 16 pot-pourri: a reference to the Modernist mixing of styles and voices used by RST in 'Border Blues', published in *Dock Leaves* 4, 11 (Summer 1953), 8–11.

p. 17 Thank you . . . for noticing 'The Minister': reviewed by RG in *Dock Leaves* 4, 11 (Summer 1953), 54–57.

p. 17 Gwydion: son and only child of RST and the distinguished artist Mildred E. (Elsi(e)) Eldridge, aged eight in August 1953. RST and Elsi had married on 5 July 1940.

p. 17 The Roman Catholics have made a pleasant church at Gellilydan: mentioned because RG was at that stage a Roman Catholic, having been received into that Church in 1948 on the eve of his marriage to Elin Hughes, a contemporary undergraduate at Bangor, who had converted as a young girl. Some thirty years later, RG was to leave the Church.

p. 18 Gwydion is in his first term at preparatory school: Packwood Haugh Preparatory School, outside Shrewsbury.

p. 18 I don't feel I have anything original I can say about Dylan Thomas: RST had been invited to contribute to *Dock Leaves*, 5, 13 (Spring 1954), a 'Dylan Thomas Number', following Thomas's death on 9 November 1953. Among the contributors, along with RG, were Louis MacNeice, Saunders Lewis, Anthony Conran, Aneirin Talfan Davies, Henry Treece, Glyn Jones and Roland Mathias.

p. 18 your poem in Time + Tide some months ago: two poems by RG had appeared in the magazine up to that point in 1953, namely 'Tenby', *Time & Tide*, 34, 47 (21 November 1953), 1519, and 'Barafundle', *Time & Tide*, 34, 48 (28 November 1953), 1540. (RG's 'Poem for Dylan' was to appear before the end of the year: *Time & Tide*, 34, 50 (12 December 1953), 1643.) RST's poem 'Invasion' (which was included in *Song at the Year's Turning* (1955) under the title 'Invasion on the Farm') had appeared in the magazine at the end of October (*Time & Tide*, 34, 44 (31 October 1953), 1422.

p. 19 your leaflet of poems: *Poems from Pembrokeshire* (Pembroke Dock: Dock Leaves Press, [1953] (Dock Leaves Pamphlet No. 2)). All but one of the poems were subsequently included in *The Welsh-Speaking Sea: Selected Poems 1949–1954* (Pembroke Dock: Dock Leaves Press, 1954).

p. 20 We have just endured a pantomime: Cf. the lines 'We still come in by the Welsh gate, but it's a long way/ To Shrewsbury now from the Welsh border . . ./ We go each Christmas to the pantomime:/ It was

Babes in the Wood this year, all about nature', from the poem 'Border Blues', which had appeared in *Dock Leaves* some months previously. The poem was subsequently published, with minor changes, in *Poetry for Supper* (1958).

p. 21 I thought – Under Milk Wood – excellent: Dylan Thomas's radio play had been broadcast by the BBC on 25 January 1954. On 2 October 1953, shortly before leaving for New York, where he died on 9 November, Dylan Thomas addressed a meeting of Tenby Arts Club, at which RG was present. Thomas gave a performance of *Under Milk Wood*, speaking all the parts himself, and it was RG who proposed the vote of thanks at the end of the meeting. See RG's account of the reading in 'Dylan Thomas and Others', *Planet*, 109 (February/March 1995), 84–85, and his poem 'The Poet Reads His Play at Tenby' in *The Welsh-Speaking Sea* (1954) ('Dylan Thomas at Tenby' in RG's *Collected Poems 1946–86* (1987)).

p. 22 Moelwyn Merchant: (1913–97) academic, poet-priest and novelist, at the time Lecturer in English at University College, Cardiff, and later (1961–74) Professor of English at the University of Exeter. Author of *R.S. Thomas* in the 'Writers of Wales' series (1979).

p. 23 Tŷ Mair: RG's house (10 Argyle Street) in Pembroke Dock, where RST and his wife Elsi had stayed overnight.

p. 24 Blaenau: Blaenau Ffestiniog, Merionethshire. RG took up the post of an Assistant English Master at Ffestiniog County School in the summer of 1954, partly so that his son Iestyn could be raised Welsh-speaking.

p. 24 Llan Ffestiniog: when RG left Blaenau Ffestiniog in 1960 he kept a cottage in Llan Ffestiniog to which the family returned annually for holidays. See also note on **I will call**, p. 173 below.

p. 24 Gildas: (*c.*495–*c.*570) monk and author of the polemic *De Excidio Britanniae* ('On the Ruin of Britain'), in which he chastises contemporary Welsh leaders – notably Maelgwn, King of Gwynedd – for their moral weaknesses. RST's reference takes its cue from his statement in the letter that the Welsh 'are an uncourageous race'. Gildas is referred to elsewhere, both directly and indirectly, in RST's prose and poetry; see Jason Walford Davies, *Gororau'r Iaith: R.S. Thomas a'r Traddodiad Llenyddol Cymraeg* (Caerdydd: Gwasg Prifysgol Cymru, 2003), 288, 305.

p. 24 Emyr Humphreys: (1919–) novelist, poet and dramatist, taught at Pwllheli Grammar School 1951–55 before joining BBC Wales as a drama producer. He was subsequently (1965–72) Lecturer in Drama at the University College of North Wales, Bangor, and thereafter a freelance writer. As it happens, RG had as an undergraduate at Bangor 'learned to recognize Emyr Humphreys – returned from the war with his first novel, *The Little Kingdom*, already under his belt'; see '1944–50: Dock Leaves and Nettles', *New Welsh Review*, 34, IX:2 (Autumn 1996), 40.

p. 25 whether you would care to have the enclosed: the poem 'On Hearing a Welshman Speak' was in time for the delayed printing of *Dock Leaves* 5, 14 (Summer 1954), 3.

p. 26 the poem pamphlet: of some poems by a former pupil of RG's at Pembroke Dock.

p. 26 We are leaving Manafon . . . for Eglwys Fach: 'Then in 1954 William Condry sent a letter to the rector [RST] to say that the vicar of Eglwys-fach was retiring, and what about it? Manafon was in the diocese of St Asaph, but the other was in the diocese of St David's. However, the former bishop of St Asaph, William Havard, was by this time bishop of St David's, and the rector wrote to him to ask to be considered as the vicar of Eglwys-fach' (from RST's autobiography *Neb* ('No-one'), written in the third person and published in Welsh in 1985; see Davies (ed. and trans.), *Autobiographies*, 62).

p. 27 Yes, include the tractor if you wish: the 'tractor' was RST's now celebrated poem 'Cynddylan on a Tractor', from *An Acre of Land* (1952).

p. 28 the copy of P.B.M.: *Poetry Book Magazine*, 6, 5 (Fall 1954) – a special *Poetry from Wales* issue – had been guest-edited by RG, who had included RST's 'Cynddylan on a Tractor'.

p. 28 Rupert Hart-Davis are bringing out Selected Poems: *Song at the Year's Turning: Poems 1942–1954* (London: Hart-Davis, 1955).

p. 29 your copy of P.B.M.: see note on **the copy of P.B.M.** above.

p. 29 your own poems: RG's *The Welsh-Speaking Sea: Selected Poems 1949–1954* (Pembroke Dock: Dock Leaves Press, 1954).

p. 29 Stockwell and Fortune are to be avoided: Arthur H. Stockwell, Ilfracombe, publisher of Roland Mathias's first volume of poetry, *Days Enduring* (1942), had not marketed the book effectively. Keidrych Rhys (see note on **Keidrych**, p. 170 below) was highly critical of Stockwell (see Sam Adams (ed.), *The Collected Poems of Roland Mathias* (Cardiff: University of Wales Press, 2002), 11). The Fortune Press, London, had published RG's first solo collection, *Poems from the Mountain-House*, in 1950.

p. 29 The last poem, Biographical Note: last, that is, in *The Welsh-Speaking Sea* (see note on **your own poems**, p. 166 above). 'Biographical Note' finely interrelates the poet's physical disability and his respect for form in poetry.

p. 29 the rest is dross: a reference to Ezra Pound's lines, 'What thou lovest well remains,/ the rest is dross/ What thou lov'st well shall not be reft from thee/ What thou lov'st well is thy true heritage' (*Pisan Cantos* LXXXI).

p. 30 whether you would like to have this: the poem, 'Commission: *for Raymond Garlick*', was in time for *Dock Leaves* 6, 17 (Summer 1955), 17. It warmly salutes RG's commitment to Wales.

p. 31 I do not take much to the cover and the printing of the title I positively dislike: the volume was *Song at the Year's Turning* (1955). Presumably, RST disliked the cover for its primitive impression of a dry-stone wall, and the cover-title for its italic print.

p. 31 my own contribution to the last D.L. [*Dock Leaves*]: RST's 'Commission: *for Raymond Garlick*' (see note on **whether you would like to have this** above).

p. 31 a Welsh Hanrahan's Song about Wales: a reference to W.B. Yeats's poem 'Red Hanrahan's Song about Ireland', from *In the Seven Woods* (1904). RST also refers to Yeats's poem in a lecture, 'Patriotism and Poetry', from the end of the 1970s; unpublished typescript in the archive of The R.S. Thomas Study Centre, Bangor University (n.d.).

p. 32 the other night on the air: 'A Poem is Made', broadcast 19 December 1955 on the BBC Welsh Home Service, in which RG explored the nature of poetic composition ('Why do people write poetry?', 'How are poems formulated in the mind?') with reference to his own work. The poems were read by Siân Phillips and John Darran, and the programme was produced by the distinguished writer and critic Dyfnallt Morgan (1917–94).

p. 32 'The Minister' is going to be done on the 3rd Program: the poem had been first broadcast on the BBC Welsh Home Service on 18 September 1952, as part of the 'Radio Odes' series. RST's American spelling of 'Program' is presumably another hint of dissatisfaction. On the BBC Third Programme broadcast in 1956, see Rhian Reynolds, 'Poetry for the Air: *The Minister*, *Sŵn y Gwynt sy'n Chwythu* and *The Dream of Jake Hopkins* as Radio Odes', *Welsh Writing in English*, 7 (2001–02), 89, 104 (n.37).

p. 32 the Welsh Reg.: the Welsh Regional Home Service.

p. 33 not at all 'dark' as Hart-Davis would have it!: in the 'Acknowledgements' statement at the head of *Song at the Year's Turning* (1955), *Dock Leaves* appeared as *Dark Leaves*. The error remained uncorrected for over a decade.

p. 33 very good of you to devote so much space to my book: in what is in many ways a seminal appraisal of RST's early stature, RG gave over the whole of his Editorial in *Dock Leaves* 6, 18 (Winter 1955) to *Song at the Year's Turning* (1955).

p. 33 trouble with our old car: for the comic saga of RST's dealings with different vehicles, see '"Quietly as Snow": Gwydion Thomas Interviewed by Walford Davies', *New Welsh Review*, 64 (Summer 2004), 34.

p. 33 Gwae ni!: 'Woe is us!'.

p. 33 your calligraphy: since the late 1950s, RG has always written in an elegant italic hand.

p. 34 I shall be pleased to take part in your discussion: the programme, entitled 'Present Indicative', was broadcast on 21 March 1956 on the BBC Welsh Home Service. In addition to an item on 'Poetry for Radio' (see RST's notes for the recording in his letter of 19 March 1956), the broadcast also included a discussion of the Welsh roots of John Cowper Powys's work and readings from the poetry of Heine.

p. 35 Elsie has the car Wednesdays and Thursdays: under the aegis of the Department of Extra-mural Studies of the University College of Wales, Aberystwyth, M.E. Eldridge was at this time teaching several highly successful classes under the running title 'The History and Appreciation of Art' at a considerable distance from Eglwys-fach – at New Quay, Barmouth, Newtown and Welshpool.

p. 36 Betjeman's remarks: John Betjeman (1906–84) had written a laudatory Introduction to *Song at the Year's Turning* (1955).

p. 37 I hope the play succeeds: as an Assistant English Master at Ffestiniog County School, RG was responsible for staging school plays. Among those produced were two of Sir Thomas Parry's works, *Lladd Wrth yr Allor* (1949) (a translation of Eliot's *Murder in the Cathedral*) and *Llywelyn Fawr* (1954).

p. 38 Bryn Awel: RG's first house in Blaenau Ffestiniog.

pp. 38–39 Radio somewhat of a return to pre-printing press days . . . ad nauseam: this material was appended to the letter of 19 March 1956 confirming RST's arrival to pick up RG for the Bangor BBC broadcast. It outlines what he planned to say on the programme (see note on **I shall be pleased to take part in your discussion**, p. 168 above).

p. 38 Ballads by Watkins: Vernon Watkins (1906–67); most famously, 'Ballad of the Mari Lwyd', the long poem which gave its name to Watkins's first volume of poetry (1941; second edition 1947). See also the Ballads in what was Watkins's most recent collection at the time, *The Death Bell* (1954).

p. 39 recordings of Tennyson: Tennyson was one of the earliest poets to be recorded reading their own poetry.

p. 40 I rehashed 'Border Blues': broadcast, with an Introduction by RST, on the BBC Third Programme on 26 November 1956, and again on 18 January 1957.

p. 40 it appeared in Dock Leaves: see note on **pot-pourri**, p. 163 above.

p. 40 this Russian business: Soviet forces had invaded Hungary on 4 November 1956.

p. 40 sub specie aeternitatis: literally, 'under the aspect of eternity' – considered in relation to the eternal.

p. 41 your little extravaganza on Bangor: 'Places of the Mind: An Appreciation of the University College of Bangor', broadcast 21 November 1956 on the BBC Welsh Home Service and produced by Dyfnallt Morgan.

p. 41 my stay there: that is, at the University College of North Wales, Bangor. RST had been an undergraduate there, studying Classics (1932–35).

p. 41 Keidrych: Keidrych Rhys (William Ronald Rees Jones, 1915–87), editor of the periodical *Wales* (1937–39/40; 1943–49; 1958–60). During its second period, it published no fewer than nineteen of RST's early poems. Keidrych Rhys was also the founder of The Druid Press at Lammas Street, Carmarthen, which published RST's first volume of poetry, *The Stones of the Field* (1946).

p. 42 Siôn Corn: Father Christmas.

p. 42 too constant a reminder of Europe: and therefore of the situation in Hungary (see note on **this Russian business**, p. 169 above).

p. 43 I hope you enjoyed Rome: RG had spent Easter 1957 in Rome. He and Elin Garlick had travelled widely in Europe, visiting Paris in 1949 and Madrid in 1951. A previous visit to Rome in the Catholic *Anno Santo* (Holy Year) of 1950 was recorded in a diary (now in the National Library of Wales) and described in RG's Editorial, *Dock Leaves*, 1, 3 (Michaelmas 1950), 1–5.

p. 43 my talk: RST had thrown away the text of his recorded Introduction to the broadcasts of 'Border Blues' (see note on **I rehashed 'Border Blues'**, p. 169 above). RG had asked to see it, with a view to publishing it in *Dock Leaves*.

p. 45 'Blaenau Observed': *Blaenau Observed: A Broadcast Poem* (Pembroke Dock: Dock Leaves Press, 1957). This poem for radio had been broadcast on the BBC Welsh Home Service on 14 June 1956. RG dedicated the published version to the novelist John Cowper Powys (1872–1963), a neighbour and friend of his at Blaenau Ffestiniog during the period 1955–60.

p. 45 a more congenial home: 'Erw Coed', Cwm Bowydd, Blaenau Ffestiniog. RG's Editorial to *Dock Leaves* 8, 22 contains a witty description of the move and of how it had delayed the publication of the magazine.

p. 45 Rome: the Roman Catholic faith.

p. 46 Sul y Blodau: Palm Sunday.

p. 46 Poetry for Supper in your editorial: RG discussed *Poetry for Supper* (London: Hart-Davis, 1958) in his Editorial to *The Anglo-Welsh Review* 9, 24, pp. 4–7, where he paid special attention to RST's poems about Iago Prytherch (described by RG as 'one of the most memorable and rounded creations of Anglo-Welsh literature' (p. 5)).

p. 46 I hope the Anglo-Welsh Review is holding its own: the title *Dock Leaves* had been changed to *The Anglo-Welsh Review* in 1957.

p. 46 I am sorry Wales started up again: the short-lived third series of Keidrych Rhys's periodical *Wales*, which ran from September 1958 to New Year 1960. RG, on the other hand, expressed a different view from that of RST: 'All who are concerned for Anglo-Welsh writing owe a debt of gratitude to Mr. Keidrych Rhys, whose magazine *Wales* provided an earlier group of now established writers with their first opportunity of appearing in print. Vigorous, catholic, controversial and colourful, its cessation has impoverished the literary scene. Its imminent return to print, under the same editor, is thus a welcome prospect: the need for a monthly magazine – with all its possibilities for experiment, contemporaneity, and the running battle of the correspondence column – requires no urging'; Editorial, *The Anglo-Welsh Review* 9, 23, pp. 7–8.

p. 46 James Hanley: (1901–85), novelist. Born in Dublin and raised in Liverpool, he moved to Wales in 1930. From 1940 to 1964 he lived in Llanfechain, Montgomeryshire, where he got to know RST. It was Hanley who recommended RST's work to Rupert Hart-Davis; *Song at the Year's Turning* (1955) was dedicated to him.

p. 47 Mr McCoye: Roye McCoye, Editor of the poetry magazine *Elegreba*, based in Abergele, Denbighshire. Several of his poems were published by RG; see, for example, *Dock Leaves*, 9, 23, pp. 52–53.

p. 49 my Christmas article: 'The Qualities of Christmas', *Wales*, 46 (November 1959), 17–20, reprinted from *Vogue*, 112, 12 (December 1956), 50–55. The article is included in Sandra Anstey (ed.), *R.S. Thomas: Selected Prose* (Bridgend: [third edition] Seren, 1995), 44–46.

p. 50 give my name: RST acted as RG's referee for various job applications. RG had applied for a teaching post at the University College of Wales, Aberystwyth.

p. 50 Gwyn Jones + Cecil Price: Gwyn Jones (1907–99), writer, scholar and critic in the field of Anglo-Welsh and Scandinavian studies; at the time Professor of English at the University College of Wales, Aberystwyth. Cecil John Price (1915–91), an expert on Drama in England and Wales, Senior Lecturer at Aberystwyth, and then Professor of English at the University College of Wales, Swansea. His article, 'The Poetry of R.S. Thomas' in *The Welsh Anvil*, 4 (1952), 82–86, is among the earliest critical engagements with RST's work.

p. 52 I am sorry you are leaving: in January 1961 RG took up a post as a teacher in the International School at Eerde Castle, in the forest of Ommen, Overijssel, in the Netherlands.

p. 52 for too many Coleridgean reasons: RST may have been thinking of the paralysis of the poetic imagination recorded in Coleridge's 'Dejection: An Ode':

> each visitation
> Suspends what nature gave me at my birth,
>   My shaping spirit of Imagination.
> For not to think of what I needs must feel
>   But to be still and patient, all I can;
> And haply by abstruse research to steal
>   From my own nature all the natural man –
>   This was my sole resource, my only plan;
> Till that which suits a part infects the whole,
> And now is almost grown the habit of my soul.

p. 54 blood and soil: from the German *Blut und Boden*, the ties of blood and native earth.

p. 54 'Cynddylan on a Tractor' going down well with children: in the anthology *Here Today: Modern Poems* (London: Hutchinson Educational, 1963), RST's 'Cynddylan on a Tractor' and 'Abersoch' appeared alongside poems by Geoffrey Hill, Thom Gunn, Charles Causley, Philip Larkin, B.S. Johnson, Stevie Smith – and Raymond Garlick ('Tenby'). The volume had an Introduction by Ted Hughes, and the selection was also issued on two records by Jupiter Recordings, London. RST and RG had recommended each other.

p. 54 'Le coeur a ses raisons': the full quotation is 'Le cœur a ses raisons que la raison ne connaît point' ('The heart has its reasons that reason knows nothing of'); Blaise Pascal (1623–62), *Pensées* (1670), IV:277.

p. 55 I will call: at RG's cottage 'Hafod' in Llan Ffestiniog, Merionethshire, bought for holiday visits from the Netherlands.

p. 56 Cummings' line: the American poet e.e. cummings (1894–1962). The quotation is from poem #35 ('how dark and single, where he ends, the earth . . .') in *No Thanks* (1935). The very volume suited RST's feeling about critics: it was self-published, and 'dedicated' to the 14 publishing houses that had turned it down.

p. 57 any chance of his coming to you: that is, to the International School at Eerde Castle in the Netherlands. The school did offer a place, but in the event it was not taken up.

p. 58 his present school: Gwydion was now at Bradfield public school. For Gwydion's own view of Bradfield, see '"Quietly as Snow": Gwydion Thomas Interviewed by Walford Davies', 29.

p. 58 Mathias' boy: Roland Mathias's son, Glyn Mathias: later Political Editor for ITN at Westminster and then Political Editor for BBC Wales in Cardiff; subsequently one of the five UK Electoral Commissioners.

p. 58 An unpleasant title: see note on **'Cynddylan on a Tractor' going down well with children**, p. 172 above. RST gleefully relishes the fact that any sequel to 'Here Today' as a title would have to be 'Gone Tomorrow'.

p. 59 do anything I can: in relation to the possibility of RG returning from the Netherlands to a post in Wales.

p. 60 about your poem: *The Anglo-Welsh Review*, 13, 32, p. 43 carried the following announcement: 'We offer our congratulations to Raymond Garlick upon the news that his poem *A Note on the Iliad*, included in No. 29 of this Review, has been selected for publication in America by the Borestone Mountain Poetry Awards in their volume *Best Poems of 1962*.

p. 60 the Inspectorate: a reference to an application RG had made in 1960, before he left for the Netherlands, to become an Inspector of Schools (RST had acted as his referee). RG was interviewed for the post at the Ministry of Education in London, but was not successful. RST's comment in this letter was, according to RG, 'a late thought, a hint that one might return to Wales'.

p. 61 tidying up at the cottage: 'Fron Deg', on the slopes of Mynydd y Rhiw, Llŷn. The cottage was part of the estate of Plas-yn-Rhiw, a small manor house bought at the end of the 1930s and restored by three sisters, Honora, Eileen and Lorna Keating, originally from Nottingham. RST had first met them in August 1954, during a visit to Bardsey Island. On RST's tenancy, and his subsequently being offered the cottage as a gift by the sisters, see his comments in Davies (ed. and trans.), *Autobiographies*, 71, 90. On the Keatings and Plas-yn-Rhiw, see Mary Allan, *The Women of Plas yn Rhiw* (Llanrwst: Gwasg Carreg Gwalch, 2005).

p. 62 the dummy of your poems: that is, the contents and outline-arrangement of RG's limited-edition *Landscapes and Figures: Selected Poems 1949–63* (London: Merrythought Press, 1964).

p. 62 'Penumbra': see the Introduction, p. xxxv above.

p. 62 a long stay in France: Marcele Karczewski, a Polish Count and exile, publisher of RST's *An Acre of Land* (1952) and *The Minister* (1953) at The Montgomeryshire Printing Company, Newtown, had moved to a *mas* outside Uzès in the Gard (Languedoc). Gwydion Thomas recalls that 'I lay in that farmhouse all one summer reading hundreds of French novels, and English ones translated in the *Livre de Poche* series' before going up to Oxford that October; see '"Quietly as Snow": Gwydion Thomas Interviewed by Walford Davies', 23.

p. 62 Lampeter wrote to me: RG had applied for a post at St David's College, Lampeter. Founded in 1822 as an independent Church of England College, in 1971 it became a constituent institution of the University of Wales.

p. 63 A certain Mr. Stephens: Meic Stephens (1938–), founding editor of *Poetry Wales* 1965–73 (RST 'Special Number', 7, 4 (Spring 1972)), and Literature Director of the Welsh Arts Council 1967–90. On RST and *Poetry Wales*, see Malcolm Ballin, 'Welsh Periodicals in English: *Second Aeon* and *Poetry Wales* (1965–1985)', *Welsh Writing in English*, 11 (2006–07), 167–71.

p. 63 seems to like his tutor: Emrys Jones (1931–), a Renaissance Literature and Shakespeare scholar, Fellow of Magdalen College, Oxford 1955–84, and Goldsmiths' Professor of English Literature 1984–98.

p. 64 your long letter: RG's letter of 20 December 1965; see the Appendix to the present volume.

p. 65 a long story behind that article: 'A Frame for Poetry', *Times Literary Supplement*, 3 March 1966, 169.

p. 65 Hogarth: RG had contacted the Hogarth Press, London regarding the possibility of their publishing a volume of his poems; see RG's letter of 20 December 1965 in the Appendix to the present volume.

p. 66 you will be returning to Wales: RG returned in 1967 to take up, from September of that year, a teaching post at Trinity College, Carmarthen.

p. 66 'Duw a'm helpo, ni fedraf ddianc rhag hon': correctly, 'Duw a'm gwaredo, ni allaf ddianc rhag hon' ('God save me, I cannot escape from this one'), the closing line of 'Hon' ('This One'), an iconic poem by T.H. Parry-Williams (1887–1975) about the inescapable cultural ties of Wales.

p. 66 Durrell: Lawrence Durrell (1912–90), novelist and poet. Durrell greatly admired Thomas's work, and both had appeared, together with Elizabeth Jennings, in the first volume of the *Penguin Modern Poets* series (1962). Durrell's phrase 'the writer's middle years' comes from the relevantly-titled 'Letters in Darkness (Belgrade): 12 January 1953' (see his *Collected Poems 1931–1974* (London: Faber and Faber, 1985), 230):

> So at last we come to the writer's
> Middle years, the hardest yet to bear,
> All will agree: for it is now
> He condenses, prunes and tries to order
> The experiences which gorged upon his youth.

p. 66 'concoct the old heroic bang': in 'Famous Poet', from *The Hawk in the Rain* (1957), Ted Hughes had described the atrophy of inspiration and poetic power:

> The autoclave of heady ambition trapped,
> The fermenting of a yeasty heart stopped –
> Burst with such pyrotechnics the dull world gaped
>   And 'Repeat that!' still they cry.
>
>   But all his efforts to concoct
> The old heroic bang from their money and praise,
> From the parent's pointing finger and the child's amaze,
> Even from the burning of his wreathed bays,
>   Have left him wrecked . . .

p. 66 Pietà: RST's *Pietà* (London: Hart-Davis, 1966).

p. 66 the slick and spiteful half truths of the columnists: RST probably had a specific review of *Pietà* in mind, namely John Carey's 'Prytherch', *New Statesman*, 17 June 1966, 894. See also the Introduction, p. xxxvii above.

p. 67 a constituency that has a nationalist member: RG was returning from Holland to a post at Trinity College, Carmarthen. Gwynfor Evans (see note on **I don't think I shall be at Pencader**, pp. 162-63 above) had been elected Plaid Cymru MP for Carmarthen on 14 July 1966.

p. 68 Euros told me that Childs listens to . . .: Euros Bowen (1904–88), poet-priest and translator. As the editor of the literary magazine *Y Fflam* ('The Flame'), he had published some of RST's early prose and poetry in Welsh. The Reverend Derrick Greenslade Childs was Principal of Trinity College, Carmarthen 1965–72, Bishop of Monmouth 1972–86 and Archbishop of Wales 1983–86.

p. 68 . . . people like Ffowc Elis and Norah Isaac: Islwyn Ffowc Elis (1924–2004), one of Wales's most influential Welsh-language novelists – at the time (1963–68) a lecturer in Welsh at Trinity College, Carmarthen. Norah Isaac (1914–2003) was Principal Lecturer in Welsh and Drama at the College.

p. 68 the saints' road to Bardsey: Ynys Enlli (Bardsey Island), according to tradition the burial place of 20,000 saints, was an important place of pilgrimage in the Middle Ages. RST was fond of recalling that three pilgrimages to Bardsey, a perilous sea crossing off the tip of the Llŷn Peninsula, equalled one to Rome.

p. 69 Aberdaron • Pwllheli: in 1967 RST became vicar of the church of St. Hywyn in Aberdaron, at the end of the Llŷn Peninsula.

p. 69 'Dach chi'n leicio yma?': 'Do you like it here?'.

p. 69 'Wrth fy modd': 'I'm very happy'.

p. 69 'Welsh Voices': *Welsh Voices: An Anthology of New Welsh Poetry* (London: J.M. Dent, 1967), edited by Bryn Griffiths (1933–), aimed primarily at representing poets born between the two World Wars. The volume included a selection of 8 poems by RST and 2 by RG.

p. 70 Eifionydd: the area between Porthmadog and Pwllheli in north-west Wales.

p. 70 This investiture: that of Prince Charles as Prince of Wales at Caernarfon Castle, July 1969.

p. 70 always the five for whose sake the city will not be destroyed: in fact in Genesis (18:23–33), God's final answer to Abraham on how many good men would make Him spare the city of Sodom is, 'For the sake of ten I will not destroy it'. RST also invokes this passage in his lecture 'Y Baich ar Ein Gwar' ('The Burden on Our Shoulders'), *Y Faner*, 30 June 1989, 14.

p. 71 the Academi has been divided into two sections: Yr Academi Gymreig, the national association of (originally, Welsh-language) writers in Wales, was established in 1959 at the instigation of the poets Waldo Williams (1904–71) and Bobi Jones (1929–). An official English-language section was founded in 1968, and RG had been asked to try to persuade RST to become a member. RST became a member of the Welsh-language section, and later one of its first Fellows.

p. 71 bois bach: literally, 'little boys', used here derogatively.

p. 72 I'm glad Gwasg Gomer are to publish your poems: RG's *A Sense of Europe: Collected Poems 1954-1968* (Llandysul: Gwasg Gomer, 1968).

p. 72 I read Elin's articles in 'Barn' for the advancement of my learning: *Barn* ('Opinion') is a monthly current affairs periodical founded in 1962 (see also note on **Alwyn Rees**, p. 184 below). Elin Garlick had, in 1968, published articles in *Barn* on subjects such as 'The Language War in Belgium', 'The State of Israel, Twenty Years Old' and 'The Revival of the Hebrew Language'. RST's comment evokes Sir Francis Bacon's title, *The Advancement of Learning* (1605).

p. 72 I'm sorry you have lost Ffowc Elis: in 1968 Islwyn Ffowc Elis (see note on **. . . people like Ffowc Elis and Norah Isaac**, p. 176 above) left his lectureship at Trinity College, Carmarthen to become (for the next three years) an editor and translator with the Welsh Books Council.

p. 72 'Not That He Brought Flowers': *Not That He Brought Flowers* (London: Hart-Davies, 1968).

p. 73 your bad news: RG's adopted son Iestyn had been diagnosed with a serious illness (aplastic leukaemia), from which, however, he was ultimately to make a total recovery.

p. 73 I will keep your Trinity students in mind: RST is presumably referring to a poetry reading at the College.

p. 74 Ffowc Elis . . . immersed in the translation business: see note on **I'm sorry you have lost Ffowc Elis**, p. 177 above.

p. 74 Miroslav Holub: (1923–98), Czech poet and immunologist.

p. 74 οἱ πολλοί: in Greek 'the many'; in English 'the common people' or 'the rabble'.

p. 75 And Prytherch, then, was he a real man?: 'And Prytherch – was he a real man . . .?' is the opening line of the poem 'Which?' in *Tares* (London: Hart-Davis, 1961).

p. 75 A Peasant: the famous RST poem beginning 'Iago Prytherch his name, though, be it allowed,/ Just an ordinary man of the bald Welsh hills', first published in 1943. On RST's depictions of Prytherch, see Patrick Crotty, 'Extraordinary Man of the Bald Welsh Hills: The Iago Prytherch Poems', in Damian Walford Davies (ed.), *Echoes to the Amen: Essays After R.S. Thomas* (Cardiff: University of Wales Press, 2003), 13–43.

p. 76 Bemerton, where 'prayer has been valid': Bemerton, near Salisbury, Wiltshire, where the poet George Herbert (1593–1633) was Rector during the last three years of his life. According to his biographer, Izaak Walton, the dying Herbert instructed that a collection of his English poems be given to his friend Nicholas Ferrar, founder of a religious community at Little Gidding, Huntingdonshire, for him to publish 'if he can think it may turn to the advantage of any dejected poor Soul'. Herbert's poems were published in 1633 as *The Temple*. The words 'prayer has been valid' ('You are here to kneel/ Where prayer has been valid') come from 'Little Gidding', the fourth of T.S. Eliot's *Four Quartets* (1943). RST's selection of Herbert's poems, *A Choice of George Herbert's Verse*, was published by Faber in 1967.

p. 77 Y Blaid: Plaid Cymru.

p. 77 Cigydd: Butcher.

p. 77 'Porth Oer': or Porthor – a bay on the north coast of the Llŷn Peninsula, not far from Aberdaron. See also RST's National Eisteddfod lecture, *Abercuawg* (Llandysul: Eisteddfod Genedlaethol Cymru, 1976), 17: 'Have we not seen Rhydlafar become Red Lava, and Penychain become Penny Chain, and Cwm Einion become Artists' Valley, and Porthor become Whistling Sands, and the Welsh content with such things?' (my translation).

pp. 77–78 No wonder signs get daubed: a key feature of the language protests of the period was the daubing of English-only road signs.

p. 78 Charlie Bach's attention to Welsh: 'Charlie Bach' ('Little Charlie') is Prince Charles, whose short period at the University College of Wales, Aberystwyth in 1969 included, diplomatically, a few lessons on the Welsh language.

p. 79 Lourdes: RG visited Lourdes at Easter 1970 (see the following letter).

p. 79 your move: RG and his family had just moved to the village of Llansteffan, Carmarthenshire. See also note on **Llansteffan**, p. 180 below.

p. 79 The ghost of Keidrych . . . at Llanybri: Keidrych Rhys (see note on **Keidrych**, p. 170 above) lived at Llan-y-bri, Carmarthenshire during the 1940s with his wife, the poet Lynette Roberts (1909–95).

p. 80 Edward Thomas wrote for something for his new venture: E.M. (Ned) Thomas (1936–), at the time Lecturer in the English Department at the University College of Wales, Aberystwyth, founded the magazine *Planet* in 1970. The first number (August/September 1970) included the poems 'Welsh Resort' and 'Farm-Hand' by RST, and 'Judgement Day' by RG. RST later became one of *Planet's* named Patrons.

p. 80 where should one go from Kierkegaard: the philosophers/theologians mentioned are Søren Kierkegaard (1813–55), Blaise Pascal (1623–62), St Augustine of Hippo (354–430), Plato (*c.*428–347 BC) and Paul Tillich (1886–1965).

p. 81 I see from the last Poetry Wales: *Poetry Wales*, 6, 1 (Summer 1970) had printed RG's 'Waterloo', 'Footnote' and 'Yours of the 29th'. In the four issues of *Poetry Wales* that year, RG was represented by 12 poems.

p. 81 to speak about Bryncroes: RST was one of several distinguished national figures who, along with parents and members of Cymdeithas Yr Iaith Gymraeg (The Welsh Language Society; see note on **Cymdeithas yr Iaith**, p. 192 below), were part of the protest in 1970 against Caernarfonshire County Council's decision to close the primary school at Bryncroes, a few miles from Aberdaron. Protesters succeeded in taking possession of the building, and for a short period an independent school was held there. The campaign to keep the school open was, however, ultimately unsuccessful, and parents were obliged to send their children to neighbouring schools.

p. 81 Western Mail: the English-language national daily newspaper of Wales. It did not print RST's letter.

p. 82 Peter Thomas: (1920–2008), at the time Secretary of State for Wales (1970–74).

p. 82 Llansteffan: Llansteffan is situated across the mouth of the river Taf from Laugharne, hence RST's droll reference to Dylan Thomas's phrase 'the heron/ Priested shore' from 'Poem in October'.

p. 83 I have signed your letter: a letter signed by RG, RST, E.M. (Ned) Thomas (1936–) and Gwyn Williams (1904–90) appeared in *The Times* under the heading 'Defenders of Welsh' on 28 May 1971, 17. The letter, sent by RG from 'Hen Ysgoldy', Llansteffan, Carmarthenshire, reads:

> Sir,
>
> We, writers of Wales in the English language, wish to identify ourselves with the continuing protest against the contemptuous injustice to the Welsh language shown by the courts, the police, and those responsible for non-bilingual road-signs. In doing so we are the voice of many in Wales known to us whose Welsh is imperfect or non-existent.

Published with this letter, under the same heading, was a robust riposte from Alwyn D. Rees (see note on **Alwyn Rees**, p. 184 below) and others to a letter in *The Times* on 25 May from Mansel Davies (1913–95) and 15 other professors from the Univeristy of Wales, condemning the activities of The Welsh Language Society.

p. 83 the rally (rali in Welsh) in Aberystwyth: RST had been billed to speak at a large rally in Aberystwyth on 24 April 1971, arranged by the newly-established Cyfeillion yr Iaith ('The Friends of the Welsh

Language') – a group formed to articulate the support of an older generation for the language campaigns of The Welsh Language Society. 50 members of the society had recently been jailed for contempt of court during a hearing in Carmarthen. Over 800 people were present at the rally in Aberystwyth, which was held in the Kings Hall and chaired by Professor Jac L. Williams (1918–77). Among the prominent figures who addressed the meeting were the novelist Marion Eames (1921–2007), the theologian R. Tudur Jones (1921–98), the poet and then minister of religion T. James Jones (1934–) and the singer and political activist Dafydd Iwan (1943–).

RG had ventured to reprove RST for not showing up at the rally in Aberystwyth. RST's anti-bilingual grounds for withdrawing are reflected even in his point about the Welsh spelling for rally being 'rali' (a reference to the word as printed in the publicity literature).

p. 83 Dafydd Orwig Jones: more commonly, Dafydd Orwig (1928–96), educationalist and local politician, later Chairman of Gwynedd Council.

p. 83 Saunders: Saunders Lewis (1893–1985), poet, dramatist and critic. The twentieth century's foremost literary and political Welsh-language figure.

p. 84 I'm sorry you are in trouble with the police: during protests and direct action in 1971 by The Welsh Language Society, RG's wife, son and sister-in-law were all arrested.

p. 84 My book will be published about March: *H'm* (London: Macmillan, 1972). RST's *Young and Old* (London: Chatto & Windus; 'Chatto Poets for the Young' series) was also published that year.

p. 85 Alwyn Gruffydd: (1951–), journalist and writer, later author of *Mae Rhywun yn Gwybod . . .* ('Somebody Knows') (Llanrwst: Gwasg Carreg Gwalch, 2004), an account of the Meibion Glyndŵr arson campaign against summer-homes in Wales.

p. 85 detention centre at Bryn Buga: Brynbuga is the Welsh name for Usk in Monmouthshire, site of the detention centre where Alwyn Gruffydd had been sentenced at the end of 1971 to 6 months' imprisonment for his part in the campaign by The Welsh Language Society against English-only road signs. Gruffydd was a partner in a recently-opened Welsh-language bookshop in Pwllheli, Llŷn.

181

p. 85 the new marriage registration laws: the statutory provision for the bilingual registration of marriages came into force on 1 April 1971. As RST notes in his third-person autobiograhy *Neb* ('No-one', 1985):

> he came to understand that the [Welsh] language had to battle on two fronts: against the oppression of the English state and its civil service; and also – the shame of it – against the Welsh themselves.
>
> He experienced a monstrous example of this when he was vicar of Aberdaron. After some patriotic Welsh people had brought pressure to bear on the government, bilingual registers were given to the Church in Wales for registering marriages, with an order from the Registrar General in London to make certain that it was English that appeared first in the register, and if the priest so wished, he could leave the Welsh out of it altogether, but not the English, on pain of death! The prejudice was clear, and R.S. protested to the Registrar General – but in vain, of course. Deanery discussions were held, and a letter was sent to the same man, with the same result. R.S. kept on protesting and encouraging more opposition; but in the next meeting of the clergymen, the Rural Dean said that he did not want to take the matter forward. In the meantime he had visited the churches and examined the registers, and nowhere but Aberdaron was registering marriages in the two languages. It was too much trouble, obviously. And there was a ready excuse to hand: you cannot keep the young couple waiting while you're rewriting the details in this old Welsh!
>
> (Davies (ed. and trans.), *Autobiographies*, 93–94)

p. 85 Peter Thomas: see note on **Peter Thomas**, p. 180 above.

p. 85 Goronwy Roberts: (1913–81), Labour MP for Caernarfon 1945–74, later Deputy Leader of the House of Lords (1975–79).

p. 86 my letter was not published: the following month, a translation of RST's unpublished letter to the *New Statesman* appeared in *Barn*, 113 (March 1972), 125. The letter criticizes the *New Statesman* for its lack of coverage of the language campaigns in Wales, and describes the treatment received by those brought before the courts as 'unfair and dangerous'. RST ends by inviting the editor of the *New Statesman* to commission 'an open-minded journalist to prepare an article on the situation so that your readers may know the true facts' (my translation).

p. 86 Goronwy Roberts: see note on **Goronwy Roberts** above.

p. 88 an answer from Macmillan's editor: disappointed with Rupert Hart-Davis, RST had placed his work with Macmillan. The first result was the volume *H'm* (see note on **My book will be published about March**, p. 181 above).

p. 88 An American publisher: it was not until 1985 that an edition of RST's poems was published by an American press. *Poems of R.S. Thomas*, which appeared from the University of Arkansas Press, was a selection of 254 poems chosen by RST himself to represent his work since 1946.

p. 89 Adfer: literally, 'to restore' – a nationalist movement that split from The Welsh Language Society. Founded in 1971, it urged support for the establishment of wholly Welsh-speaking communities in the cultural strongholds of the North and West.

p. 89 your new principal: Kenneth Mansel Jones, Principal of Trinity College, Carmarthen 1972–81.

p. 90 Better the day: evoking the old saying 'The better the day, the better the deed' because the letter was written on 'Gŵyl Ddewi' (St. David's Day).

p. 90 the Governor of Albany gaol: that is, Albany prison, Isle of Wight. In April 1970, John Barnard Jenkins (1933–), an officer in the Royal Army Dental Corps and leader of the nationalist organization Mudiad Amddiffyn Cymru ('The Movement for the Defence of Wales'), had been sentenced to ten years' imprisonment for causing a series of explosions as part of MAC's campaigns in the 1960s.

p. 90 Peter Thomas and Goronwy Roberts: see notes on **Peter Thomas** and **Goronwy Roberts**, pp. 180 and 182 above.

p. 90 Fred Francis' welcome: Ffred Ffransis (1948–), later the son-in-law of Gwynfor Evans (see note on **I don't think I shall be at Pencader**, pp. 162–63 above), sentenced to two years' imprisonment in November 1971 for direct action as part of The Welsh Language Society's campaign for a Welsh-language television channel. After his release in January 1973, Ffransis attended a series of meetings all over Wales, arranged to welcome him home.

p. 90 a selection from my 6 books by them: *Selected Poems 1946–1968* (London: Hart-Davis, MacGibbon Ltd, 1973). It was RST's own selection.

p. 91 glad to see you had won a prize!: RG's *A Sense of Time: Poems and Antipoems 1969–1972* (Llandysul: Gwasg Gomer, 1972) had won a Welsh Arts Council Literature Prize for 1973 – as had RST's *H'm* (London: Macmillan, 1972). RG's *A Sense of Europe: Collected Poems 1954–1968* (Llandysul: Gwasg Gomer, 1968) had won a Welsh Arts Council Literature Prize for 1969, as *Incense: Poems 1972–1975* (Llandysul: Gwasg Gomer, 1976) was to for 1977.

p. 92 My aged mother has just died: Margaret (Peggy) Thomas (1891–1973). On RST's difficult, but poetically creative, relationship with his domineering and over-possessive mother, see, for example, Tony Brown, *R.S. Thomas* (Cardiff: University of Wales Press, 2006), 7–9, and Katie Gramich, 'Mirror Games: Self and (M)other in the Poetry of R.S. Thomas', in Damian Walford Davies (ed.), *Echoes to the Amen: Essays After R.S. Thomas* (Cardiff: University of Wales Press, 2003), 132–48. RST's father, T.H. (Tommy) Thomas (born 1883), had died in 1965.

p. 92 gwas bach: literally, 'a little servant'; idiomatically, a servile minion.

p. 94 Saunders was saying in Cwrs y Byd: Saunders Lewis (see note on **Saunders**, p. 181 above) wrote an influential column of cultural and political journalism, 'Cwrs y Byd' ('The Course of the World' or 'Current Events'), in *Baner ac Amserau Cymru* (*Y Faner*) during the period 1939–51.

p. 94 Alwyn Rees: Alwyn David Rees (1911–74), distinguished editor and sociologist, Director of the Department of Extra-mural Studies at the University College of Wales, Aberystwyth (1949–74). Formerly that Department's Resident Tutor for Montgomeryshire (1936–46), he had got to know RST, then at Manafon. As editor (1966–74) of the periodical *Barn*, Alwyn D. Rees was a staunch supporter of the language protests of the period, and did much to further the cause of The Welsh Language Society.

p. 94 hors de combat: 'out of the fight, disabled' (OED).

p. 94 'The wrong of unshapely things . . .': 'The wrong of unshapely things is a wrong too great to be told', from W.B. Yeats's poem 'The Lover Tells of the Rose in His Heart' (*The Wind Among the Reeds*, 1899).

p. 95 John Jenkins: see note on **the Governor of Albany gaol**, p. 183 above. In 1976 RST was to express his support, along with several other important cultural figures, for a campaign to provide John Jenkins with a house on his release from prison (in June 1977). See 'Cronfa Cartref John Jenkins' ('John Jenkins's Home Fund'), *Y Faner*, 16 January 1976, 5.

p. 95 I turned the Claddagh people down: a recording of RST reading his poetry had been proposed by Claddagh Records, a label famous for its traditional Irish music catalogue and its spoken voice recordings of poets such as Robert Graves, Seamus Heaney, Patrick Kavanagh, Hugh MacDiarmid and Sorley MacLean. RST subsequently made two major recordings of his work: *R.S. Thomas Reading His Own Poems* (Welsh Arts Council Oriel Records, 1976), for which RG wrote the sleeve notes, and *R.S. Thomas Reading The Poems* (Sain Records, 1999), produced by Damian Walford Davies.

p. 95 John Montague: (1929–), Irish poet, author of *The Rough Field* (1972) and editor of *The Faber Book of Irish Verse* (1974); in 1998 he became the first holder of the Ireland Chair of Poetry. It was Montague, as one of the Directors of Claddagh Records, who had approached RST regarding the proposed recording (see previous note).

p. 96 Ficerdy Aberdaron: Aberdaron Vicarage.

p. 96 Sain Steffan: the Westminster parliament.

p. 96 what fragments I can shore against my own ruin: paraphrasing the end of T.S. Eliot's *The Waste Land*: 'These fragments I have shored against my ruins'.

p. 96 cool gales . . . no glades . . . trees . . . crowd: a humorous allusion to Alexander Pope's lines in his 'Summer: The Second Pastoral', made famous by an aria in Handel's dramatic oratorio *Semele* (1743): 'Where'er you walk, cool gales shall fan the glade,/ Trees, where you sit, shall crowd into a shade'.

p. 96 in dulce jubilo: 'In Dulci Jubilo' ('in sweet jubilation'), the title of a well-known German macaronic Christmas carol dating from the 14C, first translated into English *c.*1540.

p. 97 If our enemies force a referendum: RST correctly forecasts the 'No' result in the Welsh devolution referendum of 1 March 1979.

p. 98 very sorry to hear your news: of RG and Elin's decision to separate. Their divorce was finalised in 1982.

p. 98 eat a crazy salad with their meat: from W.B. Yeats's 'A Prayer for My Daughter' (*Michael Robartes and the Dancer*, 1921): 'It's certain that fine women eat/ A crazy salad with their meat/ Whereby the Horn of Plenty is undone'.

p. 98 mesalliances: mésalliance: 'a union between two people that is thought to be unsuitable or inappropriate' (OED).

p. 99 Y Cymric: Cymdeithas y Cymric (The Cymric Society), a Welsh-language student body at the University College of North Wales, Bangor. The Autumn term of 1976 had seen a campaign of direct action by members of The Cymric to secure greater status for the Welsh language within the institution. In November, as a result of the demonstrations, the College authorities had suspended four students – The Cymric Society's President, Secretary, Assistant Secretary and Treasurer – for the remainder of the 1976/77 academic session. The campaign to safeguard Welsh-language interests at Bangor resulted in 1976 in the establishment of Undeb Myfyrwyr Colegau Bangor (Bangor Colleges' Students Union).

p. 99 Angharad: RG's adopted daughter (see note on **a sermon on it – The adoption**, p. 163 above), who went up to Bangor the following October to study Welsh and History.

p. 99 'My Kingdom is not of this world': John 18:36, Jesus's answer before Pilate.

p. 100 your new address: RG had moved, with his daughter Angharad, into a flat close to his place of work, Trinity College, Carmarthen. See also note on **Glannant**, p. 194 below.

p. 100 that Coleg y Drindod [Trinity College, Carmarthen] stays open: at that point in the 1970s, all institutions of Further and Higher Education were under Whitehall-led funding threats.

p. 100 Thomas Blackburn: (1916–77), poet. His *The Price of an Eye* (London: Longmans, 1961) contains a brief discussion of RST's work (pp. 158–60).

p. 100 Dafydd Wigley: (1943–), Plaid Cymru MP for Caernarfon 1974–2001 (President of the party 1981–84, 1991–2000); member of the National Assembly for Wales (Caernarfon), 1999–2003 (Leader, Plaid Cymru, 1999–2000).

p. 101 a trust to buy Bardsey: the Bardsey Island Trust was incorporated under the Companies Act in December 1977, and succeeded in buying the island from Michael Pearson (Lord Cowdray) in March 1979. The aims of the trust, a registered charity, are to safeguard the island's ecosystem, to conduct scientific research on the island, to promote its cultural heritage and to protect its architectural features and archaeological sites. RST served as the first Chairman of the Bardsey Island Trust Council (1978–79).

p. 102 Sarn-y-Plas • Y Rhiw • Pwllheli: known locally as 'Sarn Rhiw', 'Sarn-y-Plas' was the cottage on the estate of Plas-yn-Rhiw to which RST moved on his retirement in 1978. See the poem 'Sarn Rhiw' in *Destinations* (Halford: Celandine Press, 1985), and RST's description of the cottage and its striking location in Davies (ed. and trans.), *Autobiographies*, 90–91.

p. 102 I want to go to Cape Clear, Cork: a previous bird-watching trip to the area had inspired the poem 'Shrine at Cape Clear' (*Not That He Brought Flowers*, 1968).

p. 102 suaviter: (Latin) 'smoothly'.

p. 103 the Ted Hughes meeting: on a short Ted Hughes poetry-reading tour of south and west Wales, the two hosts in the west were Trinity College, Carmarthen and the Department of Extra-mural Studies of the University College of Wales, Aberystwyth. The Carmarthen reading was held at the Carmarthen County Library, and was chaired by RG.

p. 104 Porth Neigwl: Hell's Mouth, a large bay at the end of the Llŷn Peninsula.

p. 107 Nov. 23 [1978]: RST's Carmarthen reading, held at the Carmarthen County Library and chaired by RG, was finally arranged for that date.

p. 107 Bedwyr and the Archbishop: Professor Bedwyr Lewis Jones (1933–92), Professor of Welsh at the University College of North Wales, Bangor 1974–92, and Gwilym Owen Williams (1913–91), Bishop of Bangor 1957–82 and Archbishop of Wales 1971–82, both members of the Bardsey Island Trust (see note on **a trust to buy Bardsey** above).

p. 109 the East window Elsie did years ago: the window was a gift to Llanpumsaint church by the Reverend Canon Walter Lloyd, Vicar of Chirk, in memory of his parents. It bears the inscription 'Adapted & made by Muriel Minter from drawings by Elsie Eldridge 1939'.

p. 109 Geraint Bowen: (1915–), poet and editor, Archdruid of the National Eisteddfod 1979–81, brother of Euros Bowen (see note on **Euros told me that Childs listens to . . .**, p. 176 above).

p. 109 Y Faner: see note on **'Y Faner'**, p. 161 above; Geraint Bowen was Editor 1977–78.

p. 109 Caerfyrddin court: Wynfford James and Rhodri Williams, two prominent members of The Welsh Language Society, had been accused of causing criminal damage at the beginning of 1977 to the television transmitter at Blaen-plwyf, Cardiganshire, and also to other broadcasting facilities in England and Wales, as part of the society's campaign for a Welsh-language televison channel. The jury had failed to reach a verdict in the trial held at Carmarthen in July 1978, and the case was heard again in November. During this second trial, the defence had argued that the composition of the jury did not accurately reflect the area's electoral rolls, claiming that there was a disproportionate number of jurors with English surnames, and also alleging that the jury had therefore not been chosen at random. The defence's request for an adjournment and a detailed statistical analysis of the situation was refused. Wynfford James (Chair of The Welsh Language Society 1975–77) and Rhodri Williams (Chair 1977–79) were sentenced to 6 months' imprisonment. Four of their supporters were jailed for a month, and another for a week, for contempt of court.

p. 109 Jonathan Gower: (1959–), journalist and writer. From 2000 until 2006 Jon Gower was BBC Wales's first Arts and Media Correspondent. Previously, he worked as a current affairs journalist for HTV and a Public Affairs Officer for the RSPB. He had first met RST in 1976 in Aberdaron through a shared interest in ornithology.

p. 110 TENEBRAE: Geoffrey Hill's fourth volume of poetry (London: Deutsch, 1978).

p. 112 ancestral voices prophesying war: from Samuel Taylor Coleridge's 'Kubla Khan': 'And 'mid this tumult Kubla heard from far/ Ancestral voices prophesying war!'.

p. 112 Bonhoeffer: Dietrich Bonhoeffer (1906–45), Lutheran pastor and theologian. His opposition to the Nazis led to his imprisonment and execution at Flossenbürg.

p. 112 Enid Pierce Roberts: (1917–), academic and scholar of medieval and early modern Welsh literature.

p. 112 Ar ôl Dewi: literally, 'after Dewi', hence the Latin 'post Davidum' at the end of the letter. But in Welsh 'Ar ôl Dewi' is a punning title because of the phrase's idiomatic meaning – '*in pursuit of* Dewi'.

p. 113 Al Purdy: Alfred Wellington Purdy (1918–2000), Canadian poet. His *Collected Poems* appeared in 1986.

p. 113 Yr Ymgyrch Gwrth-Nuclear: the Campaign for Nuclear Disarmament (CND). Established in 1958, the organization underwent a revival during the 1980s. In a letter published in *Y Faner* (see note on **'Y Faner'**, p. 161 above) on 22 May 1981 (p. 3), RST had called on taxpayers in Wales to contact their MPs to protest against their income tax being used by the government to stockpile nuclear weapons. A second letter from RST appeared in *Y Faner* on 17 July 1981 (p. 4), lamenting the fact that there had been no response to his letter of 22 May; he had also learned that he was the only one to have written to Dafydd Wigley, the MP for Caernarfon, regarding the matter. RST's reference in this letter of 16 December 1981 to what he saw as 'the apathy and willed ignorance of this area' echoes the end of his second letter to *Y Faner*, where he suggests one possible reason for the lack of support for his protest – namely that 'the majority of *Y Faner's* readers are totally heedless and are willing for the English Parliament to decide their fate' (my transation).

p. 114 John Carey: (1934–), critic and Oxford's Merton Professor of English Literature 1976–2001. In 1972, in a symposium on 'The State of Poetry' in *The Review*, Carey had remarked of the 1960s: 'A list of the decade's regrets would include the deaths of Sylvia Plath and Theodore Roethke, and the award [in 1964 by the Royal Society for Literature] of the Queen's Gold Medal for Poetry to R.S. Thomas'; *The Review*, 29/30 (Spring/Summer 1972), 64.

p. 114 Seamus Heaney: (1939–), Irish poet and critic; winner of the Nobel Prize for Literature in 1995. RST was nominated for the same prize the following year.

p. 114 (S.L.): Saunders Lewis (see note on **Saunders**, p. 181 above).

p. 114 Eheu, fugaces: Horace, *Odes*, II.xiv, 1–2: 'Eheu fugaces, Postume, Postume,/ labuntur anni' ('Ah me, Postumus, Postumus,/ the fleeting years slip by'). See also RST's poem 'Eheu! Fugaces' in *The Way of It* (1977).

p. 115 a photo of him in Y Faner: the cover of *Y Faner* on 19 November 1982 featured a photograph of the actors Iestyn Garlick, Nia Ceidiog and Beryl Williams in *Y Wers Rydd*, a three-act play televised on S4C, the Welsh-language Fourth Channel, on 20 November. S4C had been launched only a few weeks previously.

p. 115 at Llanidloes 3 weeks or so ago: in November 1982, a large rally was held in Llanidloes in support of Wayne Williams, a teacher at the local comprehensive school and Chair of The Welsh Language Society 1979–81. Williams had been sentenced in June 1981 to nine months' imprisonment for his part in the society's campaign for a Welsh-language television channel, and as a result had been dismissed from his post by the Governors of the school. He was released in December 1981. After a series of reinstatements and further dismissals, and a long period of legal action, Williams was finally fully reinstated in September 1983.

p. 115 Angharad Thomas: Angharad Tomos (1958–), political activist and leading Welsh-language novelist and prose writer. She has served as Secretary and Chair of The Welsh Language Society, and also as Editor of *Tafod y Ddraig* ('The Dragon's Tongue'), the society's magazine.

p. 115 Alwyn Rees: see note on **Alwyn Rees**, p. 184 above.

p. 115 a selection of later poems: *Later Poems 1972–1982* (London: Macmillan, 1983).

p. 115 englynion: in its most popular modern guise, an *englyn* is a concise monorhyming metrical form consisting of four lines of 10, 6, 7, 7 syllables, in full *cynghanedd*, a strict and intricate system of alliteration and rhyme.

p. 115 Yr hen Saesneg diawledig yn yr isymwybod: 'The old infernal English in the subconscious'.

p. 116 The sort of yard-sticks I have used: the poems listed are by Rimbaud, Valéry, Yeats and Eliot respectively.

p. 116 this reception in Caerdydd: at the Sherman Theatre, Cardiff, 17 May 1983, in celebration of RST's 70th birthday. The event, at which RST gave a reading, was arranged by the Academi Gymreig and introduced by the Academi's Welsh-language Section Chair, R. Gerallt Jones (1934–99). The tribute was delivered by RG.

p. 118 the Elisiaid: 'the Elises'; on his return from the Cardiff event, RST had called with Islwyn Ffowc Elis (see note on **. . . people like Ffowc Elis and Norah Isaac**, p. 176 above) at Lampeter, where Elis was by then Lecturer in Welsh (later Reader) at St David's University College.

p. 119 Mike Felton: Mick Felton (1956–), at the time Editor of Poetry Wales Press, later of Seren Books; see also the following note.

p. 119 the anthology: *Anglo-Welsh Poetry 1480–1980*, edited by RG and Roland Mathias (Bridgend: Poetry Wales Press, 1984). The selection from RST's work was as follows: 'A Peasant' (*The Stones of the Field*, 1946); 'The Welsh Hill Country', 'Cynddylan on a Tractor', 'Welsh History' (*An Acre of Land*, 1952); 'Expatriates' (*Poetry for Supper*, 1958); 'A Line from St David's' (*The Bread of Truth*, 1963); 'A Welshman at St. James' Park' (*Pietà*, 1966); 'Sir Gelli Meurig (Elizabethan)', 'Llanrhaeadr Ym Mochnant', 'Reservoirs' (*Not That He Brought Flowers*, 1968); 'Other' (*H'm*, 1972); 'The Bright Field' (*Laboratories of the Spirit*, 1975); 'The Empty Church', 'The White Tiger' (*Frequencies*, 1978).

p. 121 The Cambridge Poetry Magazine: RST's poems 'Bamboo Music' and 'Questions' were included in the magazine's 2nd Number (Spring 1984), 38–39.

p. 121 a Norwegian poet: Olav H. Hauge (1908–94), a major figure in twentieth-century Norwegian literature, born in Ulvik, western Norway, where he worked as a farmer and gardener. Several volumes of English translations of his work have been published, most recently *The Dream We Carry: Selected and Last Poems of Olav H. Hauge*, trans. Robert Bly and Robert Hedin (Port Townsend, WA: Copper Canyon Press, 2008). See also the following note.

p. 121 Fraser Steel: (1950–), at the time Poetry Editor for BBC Radio (1976–86), currently Head of Editorial Complaints at the BBC. The poetry reading referred to was part of a series held at the Arts Theatre, Covent Garden (other contributors included Geoffrey Hill and Michael Hamburger). RST read 'The Window', 'Questions', 'Unposted' and 'Pardon'. The readings were recorded and selections broadcast in a programme entitled 'Poets in Public' on BBC Radio 3 on 20 September 1984.

p. 121 yng Nghymru: 'in Wales'.

p. 122 Iestyn has Gwynfor's house: Iestyn Garlick was living in 'Talar Wen', near Llangadog, Carmarthenshire, formerly the home of Gwynfor Evans (see note on **I don't think I shall be at Pencader** pp. 162–63 above).

p. 122 Angharad Tomos: see note on **Angharad Thomas**, p. 190 above.

p. 123 the Conference . . . about a new law for the Welsh language: a national conference was held in Cardiff on 3 November 1984 to discuss The Welsh Language Society's campaign for the Welsh Language Act of 1967 to be amended in order to ensure greater legal status for the language.

p. 124 Gwilym Bangor: Gwilym Owen Williams (see note on **Bedwyr and the Archbishop**, p. 187 above).

p. 124 John Morris: (1931–), former Labour Secretary of State for Wales (1974–79), later Labour Attorney General (1997–99). In 1984 he was serving a second term as Shadow Attorney General and Principal Opposition Frontbench Spokesman for Legal Affairs (1979–81, 1983–97).

p. 124 miners . . . collecting appeals: during the miners' strike of 1984–85.

p. 124 Cymdeithas yr Iaith: Cymdeithas yr Iaith Gymraeg, The Welsh Language Society, founded in 1962. The society's various campaigns – often characterized by non-violent civil disobedience – have been instrumental in securing greater recognition and status for the Welsh Language in all aspects of public life.

p. 125 J.R. Jones: (1911–70), Welsh-language philosopher, Professor of Philosophy at University College, Swansea 1952–70.

p. 125 memorial lecture: 'Undod' ('Unity'), delivered at University College, Swansea on 9 December 1985; see Tony Brown and Bedwyr Lewis Jones (eds.), *R.S. Thomas: Pe Medrwn Yr Iaith ac Ysgrifau Eraill* (Abertawe: Christopher Davies, 1988), 139–59. A translation by Katie Gramich appears in Anstey (ed.), *R.S. Thomas: Selected Prose*, 143–58.

p. 125 Cyfeillion Llŷn: 'The Friends of Llŷn' – a pressure group co-founded by RST in 1985 to safeguard the Welshness of Llŷn by campaigning on environmental, economic and language issues. RST was the group's Secretary from 1985 to 1993.

p. 125 thoughts of an old man – but not in a dry season: contracting the first and last lines of T.S. Eliot's poem 'Gerontion': 'Here I am, an old man in a dry month' and 'Thoughts of a dry brain in a dry season'.

p. 126 the Bunker business: in 1985 Carmarthen District Council began to build an 'emergency control centre' – a nuclear bunker – near Spilman Street, not far from the town's County Hall. The construction of the underground shelter had been made possible by a 75% grant from the Conservative government of the day. Several large demonstrations against the Council's scheme were held in Carmarthen, most notably in September 1985, when peace protestors succeeded in occupying the site, and in January of the following year, when activists attempted to gain access to what was by then a heavily guarded area. This resulted in Carmarthen District Council obtaining a High Court Injunction against 17 demonstrators in March 1986. Despite widespread opposition to the bunker among local people, and condemnation of the Council's plans by several prominent figures in Wales, the scheme went ahead and the underground shelter was completed at the end of the 1980s, at an estimated cost of £400,000. However, the protests ensured that no other council in Wales subsequently adopted a similar scheme. The end of the Cold War meant that the bunker in Carmarthen was never brought into operation, and it has since been used to store paperwork. RST, a member of the Dwyfor branch of CND, describes one of his visits to the site in his diary *Blwyddyn yn Llŷn* ('A Year in Llŷn', 1990):

> Down to Carmarthen to protest against the nuclear bunker there by holding a three-hour service on Good Friday on that very spot; the guards watching us from behind the iron bars, and the big dog barking throughout. Then the big rally on the Saturday, when thousands came together and encircled the bunker itself. At one o'clock everyone fell down feigning death, as a warning of how it would be after a nuclear attack. I heard of the bravery of some of the members of the anti-nuclear movement, who still challenge the unspeakable authorities by breaking in and being bitten by dogs, or abused by the guards. Then back to the silence of Llŷn, where the sea still breaks on the beach, as it did before man was created, and as it will do after a nuclear war. From the world of man back to the world of nature, with me unworthy of the bravery of the one and of the beauty of the other.

> (Davies (ed. and trans.), *Autobiographies*, 128)

193

p. 126 Breudeth: a peace protest had been held at the U.S. naval station in Brawdy, Pembrokeshire, a facility established in 1975 for the tracking of submarines. The station was closed in 1995.

p. 126 I stayed the night with Gwynfor . . .: Gwynfor Evans (see note on **I don't think I shall be at Pencader**, pp. 162–63 above) and his wife Rhiannon had moved in the summer of 1984 to a house in Pencarreg, Carmarthenshire, for which they retained the name 'Talar Wen'.

p. 126 . . . the others stayed with Guto Prys: Guto Prys ap Gwynfor (1948–), Gwynfor Evans's son, at the time a minister of religion in Lampeter, Cardiganshire. With his wife Siân he played a leading role in the protests against Carmarthen District Council's nuclear bunker (see note on **the Bunker business**, p. 193 above).

p. 126 Trawsfynydd: the twin-reactor Magnox nuclear power station at Trawsfynydd, Merionethshire, had been operational since 1965, generating electricity for the National Grid. It ceased operating in 1991, and is currently being decommissioned.

p. 127 'Cyfeillion Llŷn': see note on **Cyfeillion Llŷn**, p. 192 above.

p. 128 your selection: RG's *Collected Poems 1946–86* (Llandysul: Gwasg Gomer, 1987).

p. 128 Glannant: 'Tŷ Glannant', College Road – RG's home in Carmarthen.

p. 128 got drawn into CADNO: an action group, established in November 1987, which opposed the plan to build a Pressurised Water Reactor ('P.W.R.') nuclear power station in Trawsfynydd, Merionethshire.

p. 128 H. Pritchard Jones: Harri Pritchard Jones (1933–), novelist and short story writer, currently Welsh-language Chair of the Welsh Academy.

p. 128 the Union of Welsh Writers: founded in 1982, the Welsh Union of Writers helped authors to secure grants, publishing contracts and media coverage of their work. The Union was formally disbanded in 2004. A transcript of RST's lecture and the ensuing discussion was printed as 'Language, Exile, a Writer and the Future' in *The Works*, 1 (1988), 22–43.

p. 128 in Harlech: at Coleg Harlech, the Adult Education College founded in 1927. The Welsh Union of Writers had held their annual conference there in September 1987.

p. 129 Belinda Humfrey: (1938–), at the time Senior Lecturer in English at St David's University College, Lampeter; founding editor in 1988 of *The New Welsh Review*, a successor to *The Anglo-Welsh Review*, which ceased that year.

p. 129 bondigrybwyll: 'hardly mentionable', 'blasted'.

p. 129 Byd ar Bedwar: *Y Byd ar Bedwar* (literally, 'The World on Four'), a current affairs television programme on S4C, the Welsh-language Fourth Channel. The edition of the programme on which RST appeared was televised on 29 February 1988. In the interview – which took as its theme the contemporary state of the Welsh nation – RST had discussed the arson campaign of the nationalist group Meibion Glyndŵr (The Sons of Glyndŵr) against English-owned holiday and second homes in Welsh-speaking areas. RG recalls replying that he disagreed with the second of the two points that RST was complaining had been cut – hence RST's letter of 27 May 1988 (see note on **You must know what I am trying to do in Wales** below).

p. 130 your letter and its enclosure: RG had urged RST to support *The New Welsh Review* (see note on **Belinda Humfrey** above).

p. 130 the eastern Mediterranean: in the years immediately after his retirement from teaching at Trinity College, Carmarthen in 1986, RG went on three Swan Hellenic cruises to some of the great archaeological sites of the Classical world – visits that were a major source of inspiration for the poems published in *Travel Notes* (Llandysul: Gwasg Gomer, 1992).

p. 131 the good news of Angharad: the birth of a daughter, Alys.

p. 131 You must know what I am trying to do in Wales: a response to RG's reply to the letter of 5 March 1988 disagreeing with RST's point that 'even if one Englishman got killed, what is that compared with the killing of our nation?' (see note on **Byd ar Bedwar** above).

p. 131 Malvinas: the Falkland Islands, over which Britain went to war against Argentina (April–June 1982).

p. 132 devices through the letter-boxes of estate agents: in 1988 Meibion Glyndŵr (see note on **Byd ar Bedwar** above) started targeting the offices of estate agents in Wales. Companies in England that sold property in Wales were also attacked, with incendiary devices being posted through the letter-boxes of estate agents in numerous towns and cities, including Chester, Shrewsbury, Liverpool, Telford, Bristol, Worcester and London.

p. 132 Dylan Iorwerth: (1957–), journalist and founder-editor of the Welsh-language weekly magazine *Golwg*, established in 1988.

p. 133 I strung them on a length of prose: each poem in *The Echoes Return Slow* (London: Macmillan, 1988) faces a prose 'equivalent'.

p. 134 grandchild: see note on **the good news of Angharad**, p. 195 above.

p. 134 Peter Walker: (1932–), Conservative politician, at the time Secretary of State for Wales (1987–90).

p. 134 the Merriman Society: founded in 1967, the society commemorates the eighteenth-century Irish poet Brian Merriman (*c.*1749–1805) and is dedicated to the promotion of Irish culture.

p. 134 Cathleen ni Houlihan: a personification of cultural-nationalist Ireland, as in W.B. Yeats's play *Cathleen ni Houlihan* (1902).

p. 134 Elin ap Hywel: (1962–), Welsh poet, writer and translator.

p. 134 The Midnight Court: *Cúirt an Mheán Oíche* (*c.*1780), Brian Merriman's long Rabelaisian poem.

p. 135 your travels: RG had visited Troy in June 1989.

p. 135 Llywelyn's castle at Dolwyddelan: situated overlooking the Lledr Valley in Caernarfonshire. The square stone keep that can be seen today was built by Llywelyn ab Iorwerth (Llywelyn Fawr ('The Great'), *c.*1173–1240), who was, according to a tradition going back to the end of the 16C, born in an earlier castle near the present site.

p. 136 Here is my effort: the poem was published, with minor changes of phrasing and punctuation, as 'Postcard' in RST's posthumous collection, *Residues* (Tarset: Bloodaxe Books, 2002), 48.

p. 137 the outbursts in Europe: the upheavals and revolutions of 1989, and the fall of the Berlin Wall in November that year, signalled the dismantling of the communist regimes of Central and Eastern Europe, the break-up of the Soviet Union and the end of the Cold War.

p. 137 yng Nghymru: 'in Wales'.

p. 137 Saunders and Alwyn Rees: see notes on **Saunders** and **Alwyn Rees**, pp. 181 and 184 above.

p. 137 Cyfeillion Llŷn: see note on **Cyfeillion Llŷn**, p. 192 above.

p. 138 so glad to hear you were writing poetry again: after ten years' silence as a poet (1979–89), RG had been prompted to start writing again by a BBC 'Bookmark' documentary on W.B. Yeats, televised on 7 March 1989; see RG's 'A Poet Looks Back', *Book News from Wales* (Summer 1989), 4–5, and his comments in David Lloyd, 'An Interview with Raymond Garlick', *Poetry Wales*, 26, 3 (January 1991), 42 (the interview was republished in David T. Lloyd, *Writing on the Edge: Interviews with Writers and Editors of Wales* (Amsterdam & Atlanta, GA: Rodopi, 1997), 23–31). Also relevant is RG's poem 'After George Herbert' in *Travel Notes* (Llandysul: Gwasg Gomer, 1992), 9.

p. 139 Saesneg in Rhuddlan: 'English in Rhuddlan'. The postcard shows a painting by English landscape artist John Varley (1778–1842) of the interior of '"Blackmoor Head", Rhuddlan', dated 1803.

p. 140 glad to see you are writing again: RG's poem 'Patmos' had appeared in the December 1990/January 1991 issue of *Planet*.

p. 140 'Let us endure an hour and see injustice done': from poem XLVIII of A.E. Housman's *A Shropshire Lad* (1896):

> Now, and I muse for why and never find the reason,
> I pace the earth, and drink the air, and feel the sun.
> Be still, be still, my soul; it is but for a season:
> Let us endure an hour and see injustice done.

p. 142 Ealing College: by this time, Ealing College of Higher Education had in fact, along with three other colleges, become the Polytechnic of West London (later Thames Valley University).

p. 142 Sharon and Rhodri: Sharon (née Young) was Gwydion's second wife, and mother of their son Rhodri.

p. 144 'There's no use complaining . . .': from W.B. Yeats's poem 'The Curse of Cromwell' (*New Poems*, 1938):

> All neighbourly content and easy talk are gone,
> But there's no good complaining, for money's rant is on,
> He that's mounting up must on his neighbour mount
> And we and all the Muses are things of no account.

197

p. 145 any huckster's loins: from W.B. Yeats's introductory poem to *Responsibilities* (1914): 'Merchant and scholar who have left me blood/ That has not passed through any huckster's loin'.

p. 145 glad to see from 'Planet' that you are publishing again: *Planet*, 96 (December 1992/January 1993) had carried a review by Wyn Binding of RG's new volume of poetry, *Travel Notes* (Llandysul: Gwasg Gomer, 1992).

p. 146 I was born at the end of the month: RST's birthdate was 29 March 1913.

p. 146 that poem . . . congratulating the old thing for living so long: 'Ninetieth Birthday' (*Tares*, 1961): 'You bring her greeting/ And praise for having lasted so long/ With time's knife shaving the bone'.

p. 146 'I had forgiven enough, that had forgiven old age': from W.B. Yeats's poem 'Quarrel in Old Age' (*The Winding Stair and Other Poems*, 1933).

p. 146 John Wain . . . seems to have begun it: in 'On the Breaking of Forms', one of his lectures as Oxford's Professor of Poetry 1973–78, poet, novelist and critic John Wain (1925–94) had criticized what he saw as a 'flight from form' in RST's 1972 collection, *H'm*; see John Wain, *Professing Poetry* (Harmondsworth: Penguin Books, 1978), 107–8, and the following note.

p. 146 Donald Davie: (1922–95) poet, critic and academic, author of *Purity of Diction in English Verse* (1952) and *Articulate Energy* (1955). RST is here referring to Davie's 'R.S. Thomas's Poetry of the Church of Wales', a 1987 essay that begins by quoting Wain's comments on RST's so-called 'flight from form'. The piece was reprinted in William V. Davis (ed.), *Miraculous Simplicity: Essays on R.S. Thomas* (Fayetteville: University of Arkansas Press) – a volume which, in March 1993, had just been published to coincide with RST's eightieth birthday that month (hence 'I am receiving various essays + reviews' earlier in the letter).

p. 146 Larkin: Philip Larkin (1922–85), poet and Librarian of Hull University.

p. 147 the Caerdydd Festival: RST's *Collected Poems 1945–1990* (1993) was launched on 6 October 1993 at the Cardiff Royal Hotel as part of the Cardiff Literature Festival. For two amusing anecdotes relating to the launch, at which RST gave a reading, see Peter Finch,

Real Cardiff (Bridgend: Seren, 2002), 58, and M. Wynn Thomas, 'R.S.', *Barddas*, 260 (December/January 2000–01), 18–19.

p. 147 to be near some friends: see following note.

p. 148 to be near some former friends to help them: Betty Kirk-Owen (1916–), an Irish-Canadian, and Richard Vernon were by this stage married. They had been RST's parishioners and neighbours for a period at Eglwys-fach. In August 1996, Betty Vernon became RST's second wife.

p. 148 an anthology of Forward poetry: the Forward Poetry Prizes were launched in 1991 to highlight contemporary poets, both new and established. RST had been sent a copy of *The Forward Book of Poetry 1994* (London: Forward Publishing, 1993), which included his poem 'Plas-yn-Rhiw', from *Mass for Hard Times* (1992).

p. 149 Cefn Du Ganol • Llanfairynghornwy: RST and Betty had rented a house on the north-west coast of Anglesey, not far from Holyhead, RST's childhood home.

p. 149 I had not foreseen this move: in his autobiography *Neb* ('No-one', 1985), RST had described reaching Aberdaron (in 1967) as the culmination of his 'personal pilgrimage'. The Anglesey of his childhood, however, still exerted a powerful influence on him: 'Standing on the summit of Mynydd Mawr on a fine day, he could see Holyhead in the north and imagine himself as a child forty years before, playing on the beach there. Forty years distant in time, and only forty miles the distance'. RST's return, late in life, to Anglesey represented the completion of the 'oval' his career had traced; see Davies (ed. and trans.), *Autobiographies*, 77.

p. 150 Questions to the Prophet: the poem had appeared in *Mass for Hard Times* (Newcastle upon Tyne: Bloodaxe Books, 1992), 22.

p. 151 a paradox of Zeno: Zeno of Elea (*c*.490–*c*.420 BC), known for his series of paradoxes. Lines 7–8 of RST's poem allude to the paradox of Achilles and the Tortoise, which, by defining a race between the two in terms of an infinite number of fixed points, concludes that if the tortoise is given a head start, Achilles will never be able to catch up with it, no matter how fast he runs. By the time he has run the distance between each point, the tortoise will have moved on, and thus Achilles will always have further to travel. RST may also have in mind Aesop's famous fable of the hare and the tortoise.

p. 152 A visit to Catalunya: RST gave a reading at a conference in Barcelona which had been arranged by Wales Arts International. Other writers in the Welsh delegation included Angharad Tomos (see note on **Angharad Thomas**, p. 190 above), Dannie Abse (1923–), Gareth Alban Davies (1926–2009), Steve Griffiths (1949–), Menna Elfyn (1951–) and Gwyneth Lewis (1959–).

p. 152 the so-called ceasefire: a ceasefire had been announced by the IRA on 31 August 1994, and by the Combined Loyalist Military Command on 13 October that year. However, no agreement had been reached regarding the decommissioning of paramilitary weapons, and on 9 February 1996 the bombing of London's Docklands signalled the end of the 17-month IRA ceasefire.

p. 152 Iain Crichton Smith: (Iain Mac a'Ghobhainn, 1928–98) Scottish poet, novelist and short story writer, in both Gaelic and English.

p. 152 'I grow old' . . .: from T.S. Eliot's 'The Love Song of J. Alfred Prufrock', *Prufrock and Other Observations* (1917).

p. 153 Harper Collins: publishers in 1996 of a life of RST by Justin Wintle – *Furious Interiors: Wales, R.S. Thomas and God.*

p. 153 the book on you: *Raymond Garlick* (Cardiff: University of Wales Press ('Writers of Wales' series), 1996) by Don Dale-Jones, a former colleague of RG's in the English Department at Trinity College, Carmarthen.

p. 153 I re-married in August: RST's second wife was Betty Vernon. See note on **to be near some former friends to help them**, p. 199 above.

p. 155 U.A.E.: United Arab Emirates.

p. 155 Munich . . . to receive a prize: the Horst Bienek Prize for Poetry from the Bavarian Academy of Fine Arts.

p. 155 Kevin Perryman: (1950–), poet, translator and, since 1983, editor of the periodical *BABEL*. His editions and translations of RST's poetry, published by *BABEL*, include *Das Helle Feld/The Bright Field* (1995), *Laubbaum Sprache/Deciduous Language* (1998), *Die Vogelscheuche Nächstenliebe/Charity's Scarecrow* (2003) and *Steinzwitschern/ Stone Twittering* (2008). On the reception of R.S. Thomas's work in the

German-speaking world, see Johannes Gramich, 'R.S. in Munich', *New Welsh Review*, 54 (XIV, II), Autumn 2001, 20–23.

p. 156 Siôn Aubrey: Siôn Aubrey Roberts (1972–), arrested in December 1991, convicted in March 1993 of sending explosive devices through the post as part of the Meibion Glyndŵr (The Sons of Glyndŵr) summer-homes arson campaign in Wales, and sentenced to twelve years' imprisonment. He was released in December 1997.

p. 156 a selection of your poems: RST may have been thinking mistakenly of the anthology *Twentieth-century Anglo-Welsh Poetry*, edited by Dannie Abse and published by Seren Books in 1997.

p. 156 Alice: see RST's 'To a Lady' in *No Truce with the Furies* (1995) and 'For Alice' in *Six Poems* (1997). The former book was dedicated to Alice.

p. 156 Swan Hellenic: see note on **the eastern Mediterranean**, p. 195 above.

p. 156 in Luxor two days before the massacre: on 17 November 1997, Islamic extremists massacred 62 people at the temple of Queen Hatshepsut in Luxor, Egypt.

p. 157 Tŷ Main: a cottage owned by the Clough Williams-Ellis Foundation, situated on its Brondanw estate in Merionethshire.

p. 157 Annwyl: 'Dear'.

p. 157 Eifionydd: see note on **Eifionydd**, p. 177 above.

p. 157 Ardudwy: the area between the rivers Glaslyn and Mawddach.

p. 158 Twll y Cae • Pentrefelin: RST's last address lies between Porthmadog and Cricieth in north-west Wales.

Translation of Welsh valedictions (alphabetical) at the end of letters:

Bendithion lawer = Many blessings; *Blwyddyn newydd dda a phob bendith* = A happy new year and every blessing; *Blwyddyn newydd well* = A better new year; *Cofion* = Regards; *Cofion caredig* = Kind regards; *Cofion cu* = Affectionate regards; *Cofion cu a phob bendith* = Affectionate regards and every blessing; *Cofion cynnes* = Warm regards; *Cofion cynnes at 1970* = Warm regards for 1970; *Cofion fil* = (literally) A thousand regards; *Cyfarchion Nadolig* = Christmas greetings; *Gwyliau llawen* = Happy holidays; *Gyda chyfarchion* = With greetings; *Gyda dymuniadau cu* = With affectionate wishes; *Gyda phob dymuniad da i chi yn y flwyddyn newydd* = With every good wish to you in the new year; *Nadolig dedwydd* = A blessed Christmas; *Nadolig dedwydd i chi i gyd* = A blessed Christmas to you all; *Nadolig llawen i chwi i gyd* = A happy Christmas to you all; *Pob bendith* = Every blessing; *Pob bendith arnoch eich tri yn ystod gŵyl eni'r Iesu* = Every blessing on the three of you during the festival of Jesus's birth; *Yn bur* = Sincerely; *Yn bur iawn* = Very sincerely; *Yn garedig* = With kind wishes; *Yn gynnes* = Warmly.

GLOSSARY OF WELSH PLACE-NAMES MENTIONED IN THE LETTERS

Abergwaun	Fishguard
Abertawe	Swansea
Breudeth	Brawdy
Bryn Buga (Brynbuga)	Usk
Caerdydd	Cardiff
Caerfyrddin	Carmarthen
Caergybi	Holyhead
Caerlleon (Caerllion)	Caerleon
Cernyw	Cornwall
Cwm Croesor	The Croesor Valley
Cymru	Wales
Llanbedr Pont Steffan	Lampeter
Llanhenog (Llanhenwg)	Llanhennock
Meironnydd	Merioneth
Morgannwg	Glamorgan
Penfro	(as used by RST in his letter on p. 10) Pembrokeshire
Porth Neigwl	Hell's Mouth
Sir Aberteifi	Cardiganshire
Ynys Enlli	Bardsey Island
Ynys Môn	Anglesey
Yr Wyddfa	Snowdon

APPENDIX:
RAYMOND GARLICK'S ONLY SURVIVING
LETTER TO R.S. THOMAS

Kruupweg 2 • Eerde • Ommen • The Netherlands
20th December 1965

Dear Ronald,

These Christmas greetings come to you from a waterlogged countryside of broken dykes and sprawling rivers, & even the deer are splashing about the forest. Happily we are above flood-level here. Everyone is hoping for a cold spell to freeze out the rain – not least Iestyn, who has a new pair of skates.

I have spent this term reading Teilhard de Chardin & Claude Lévi-Strauss, the latter's work being the most influential in France at the moment. His 'Tristes Tropiques' – translated into English under the same title – is a fascinating book: a kind of general critique of ideas, taking as its foundation the Indian anthropology of Brazil, on which the author is one of the principal experts. It is, however, a literary work, & even in English the structure & style are impressive.

The other day a friend of mine called Hugo van Eysselsteyn was here. He is a composer & professional musician. He had with him some songs he had just finished, & three of them were settings of your 'Pisces', 'Song for Gwydion' and 'Madrigal'. He was talking about sending the whole lot to a London music-publisher, or to the BBC. I said that I imagined copyright would be involved, & told him to write to Hart-Davis. I mention all this so that, if it reaches you, you will at least know he is a reputable person and, I am told, a promising composer. I know nothing of music.

Oxford University Press wrote me an extraordinarily encouraging report on a collection of poems they had agreed to look at, & though they wouldn't take them I was cheered by what their readers said. The Hogarth Press has said it will have a look at a collection now.

A month or so ago the Netherlands Television News included a report of Tryweryn, in which we observed Robert Wynne of Garthewin being carried off by the police. A few weeks later we heard that the same fate had befallen John Daniel in the Dolgellau Post Office episode. All this makes Iestyn anxious to join the fracas at home.

At the end of the month we shall have completed five years here. This was the period for which the Ministry of Education allowed me to absent myself while remaining in their superannuation scheme. They have extended this for one final year – to enable me to discharge obligations here & return, if I intend to. On the whole, my inclination is not to do so. If interesting work were to turn up, I suppose I should consider it. But since I couldn't get anything else in Wales in 1960, I see no reason to expect it now. There is no question, in any case, but that leaving here would involve very considerable sacrifices – not least the awareness that one really is wanted & needed.

So, warm greetings for Christmas & the New Year from us all:

Yours,

Raymond

NOTES AND REFERENCES TO THE APPENDIX

p. 203 Kruupweg 2 • Eerde • Ommen • The Netherlands: see note on **I am sorry you are leaving**, p. 172 above.

p. 203 Teilhard de Chardin: Pierre Teilhard de Chardin (1881–1955), French philosopher, palaeontologist and Jesuit priest; author of *Le Phénomène humain* ('The Phenomenon of Humanity', 1955).

p. 203 Claude Lévi-Strauss: (1908–), French social anthropologist and one of the seminal figures of Structuralism. See RG's poem 'After Lévi-Strauss' in *A Sense of Europe* (1968).

p. 203 'Tristes Tropiques': Lévi-Strauss's influential book was first published in 1955. In an essay on his friendship with John Cowper Powys (1872–1963) and Phyllis Playter (1894–1982), Powys's lifelong companion (the couple had settled in Blaenau Ffestiniog, Merionethshire in 1955), RG notes: 'When – home on holiday from the Netherlands in 1964 – I talked with enthusiasm about *Tristes Tropiques* by Claude Lévi-Strauss, which we were all reading there, Phyllis was the only person I found who was familiar with his ideas'; see 'Mr Powys and Miss Playter', *Planet*, 110 (April/May 1995), 56.

p. 203 Hugo van Eysselsteyn: Hugo van Eysselsteyn Kummer (1927–), Dutch musician whose compositions include choral works and chamber music. In addition to the settings of poems by RST mentioned here, van Eysselsteyn also composed songs based on works by C. Day Lewis, Thomas Hardy and RG himself; see <http://www.donemus.nl/componist.php?id=119&lang=EN>, accessed 23 August 2008.

p. 203 Tryweryn: In 1955, the Liverpool Corporation had announced its intention to create a reservoir in the Tryweryn valley, near Y Bala, Merionethshire, to provide water for the city, thereby drowning the village of Capel Celyn and several farms in the area. A parliamentary bill for this purpose was given royal assent in 1957, despite not having been supported by Welsh MPs in the House of Commons. The proposed destruction of the Welsh-speaking community of Capel Celyn met with considerable opposition in Wales in the form of a concerted campaign by Plaid Cymru, widespread public condemnation and, in the early 1960s, the sabotaging of electrical transformers on the site. Such protests, however, proved fruitless, and by the summer of 1965 the valley had been drowned. The reservoir, Llyn Celyn, was officially opened on 21 October 1965. On 19 October 2005, Liverpool City Council issued an official apology to the people of Wales for the events of 1955–65.

p. 203 Robert Wynne of Garthewin being carried off by the police: R.O.F. Wynne (1907–93), nationalist and squire of Garthewin, an 18th-century mansion in Llanfair Talhaearn, Denbighshire. A barn on the estate was adapted by Thomas Taig in 1937 for use as a theatre, where several important plays by Wynne's close friend and fellow Roman Catholic, Saunders Lewis (see note on **Saunders**, p. 181 above), were performed for the first time. In 1963 Wynne had chaired a committee to establish a fund for Owain Williams and John Albert Jones, who had been responsible for acts of sabotage at the site of the Tryweryn reservoir and later at Gellilydan, Merionethshire. He had also donated £500 to free the two on bail. The ceremony to mark the official opening of the reservoir on 21 October 1965 was disrupted by a large protest, at which the police removed demonstrators who had attempted to block the path of cars carrying guests and dignitaries.

p. 203 John Daniel: John (Siôn) Illtud Daniel (1937–2005), philosopher and political activist. He lectured in philosophy at Aberystwyth 1964–66, Bangor 1969–85, and Lampeter 1985–2003, and was, from 1963 to 1965, the first Chair of The Welsh Language Society (serving as its Secretary 1965–67).

p. 203 the Dolgellau Post Office episode: On 27 November 1965, The Welsh Language Society held a sit-in demonstration at the post office in Dolgellau, Merionethshire, to protest against the GPO's refusal to afford equal status to the Welsh language in its official business. Having been forcibly removed from the post office by the police, several demonstrators were set upon by a group of local people.